ANTHROPOLOGICAL PAPERS

MUSEUM OF ANTHROPOLOGY, UNIVERSITY OF MICHIGAN

NO. 36

THE NAOMIKONG POINT SITE AND THE DIMENSIONS OF LAUREL IN THE LAKE SUPERIOR REGION

BY

DONALD E. JANZEN

ANN ARBOR

THE UNIVERSITY OF MICHIGAN, 1968

PREFACE

ON August 12, 1967, an archaeological crew from the University of Michigan Museum of Anthropology returned to Ann Arbor. They were bearded, dirty, and tired. This was the final chapter in two seasons of excavations at the Naomikong Point site on the south shore of Lake Superior. By July 8, 1968, the enormous quantity of material which had been recovered at Naomikong Point was washed, catalogued, and analyzed, and the site report was written.

The gap between the dirty archaeologist and the final manuscript is filled with a large number of hard-working people whose efforts hastened the completion of the task. While only my name is attached to this manuscript I would like to acknowledge these individuals and express my thanks for their services. The following students at the University of Michigan were enrolled in the Museum Techniques Program and provided invaluable assistance: Jan Carline, Peter Doren, Michael Gilmartin, Anita Fahringer, Jane Hartough, Jane Hollander, Roberta Lev, Melinda Main, Colleen McLean, Andrea Moore, Elaine Pearson, Richard Redding, Diane Saltz, Elizabeth Taylor, Lyn Wiley, and Mary Lynn Woodruff. Miss Bea Bigony washed and catalogued the material from the 1966 excavations, Mrs. Vickie Rosenblum and Mr. Jan Carline analyzed the flint chippage and Mr. Dan Caister analyzed the historic material. Mr. Burton Barnard of Wayne State University drew the site map and Mr. George Stuber directed the photographic work.

I wish to thank the members of my Doctoral committee for directing me in my research and for valuable criticism of the manuscript. My chairman Dr. James E. Fitting, and Dr. James B. Griffin, of the Museum of Anthropology, were particularly helpful in this respect. I take full responsibility, however, for any errors or shortcomings.

Frances Steketee typed the rough draft and final copy of the dissertation. This one simple sentence hardly does justice to the important role played by Miss Steketee. Mrs. Joanne Bailis edited the manuscript and Misses Elizabeth Keller and Barbara Becker proofread the final copy. Finally, I wish to thank Martha, my wife, whose patience and support is deeply appreciated.

This research was supported by the National Science Foundation Grant (GS-1486).

Contents

I

INTRODUCTION

HISTORY OF INVESTIGATIONS

NAOMIKONG Point and Menekaunee Point are twin points of land on the south shore of Lake Superior in the Upper Peninsula of Michigan. They are located in section 9 (T.47N, R.5W) of Bay Mills Township in Chippewa County. Although these are two distinct points, they are situated at the end of a larger point and the entire area is commonly called Naomikong Point (Fig. 1 and 2). The presence of an archaeological site in this region has been known for many years by both professional archaeologists and local amateurs. The earliest reference to Naomikong Point as an archaeological site appears in W. B. Hinsdale's *Archaeological Atlas of Michigan* (1931). Emerson F. Greenman surveyed the area east of Naomikong Point in the vicinity of Iroquois Island in 1939 and visited the site at that time. No excavations were conducted and only a few sherds were collected from the beach (Greenman, personal communication).

In 1963 the site was reintroduced to archaeologists by Mr. Charles S. Taylor of Newberry, Michigan. Recognizing the potential of the site, he contacted George I. Quimby of the Chicago Natural History Museum regarding possible excavation. The next fall Taylor took Quimby to the area and showed him collections from the site. This stimulated new interest, and in the spring of 1965 Quimby and James E. Fitting of the University of Michigan Museum of Anthropology planned a joint survey of the site. On the evening of June 18, 1965, James E. Fitting and I, representing the University of Michigan, met with George Quimby and James Getz of the Chicago Natural History Museum in Paradise, Michigan to review plans for the survey. It was necessary to apply for permission to dig a test trench since the site is within the Hiawatha National Forest and federal laws prohibit excavation without a permit. Unfortunately the application had not been processed by the time of this meeting, and it was therefore decided to limit the survey to a surface collection from the beach, and an underwater collection from the lake. The next day the survey team proceeded to the site accompanied by a group of

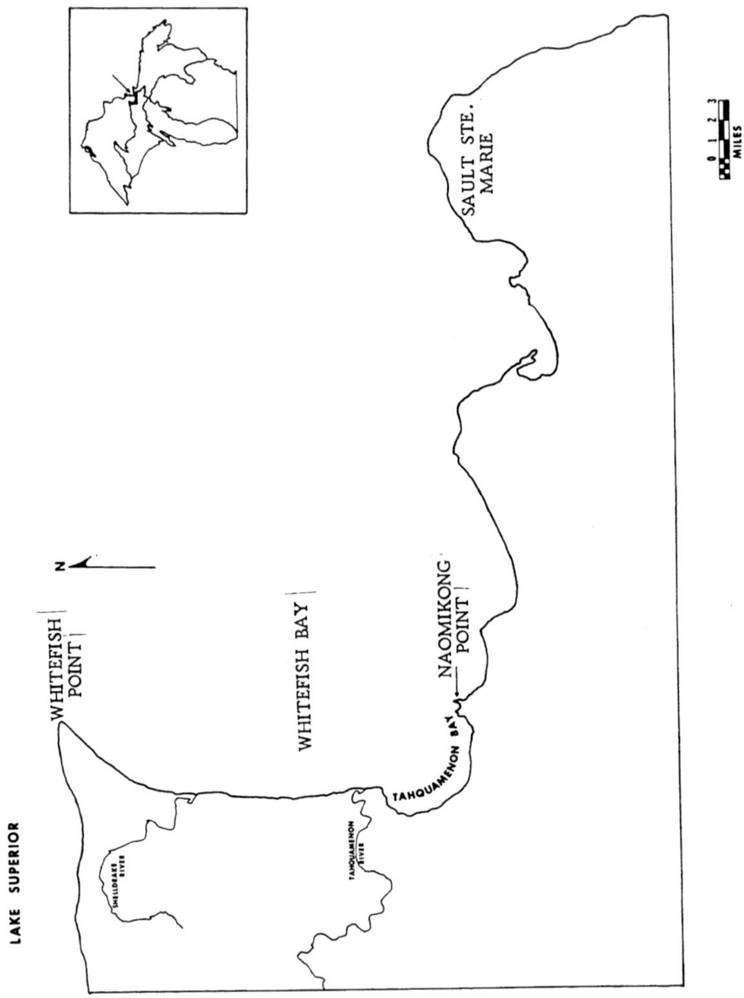

FIG. 1. Whitefish Bay area showing Naomikong Point.

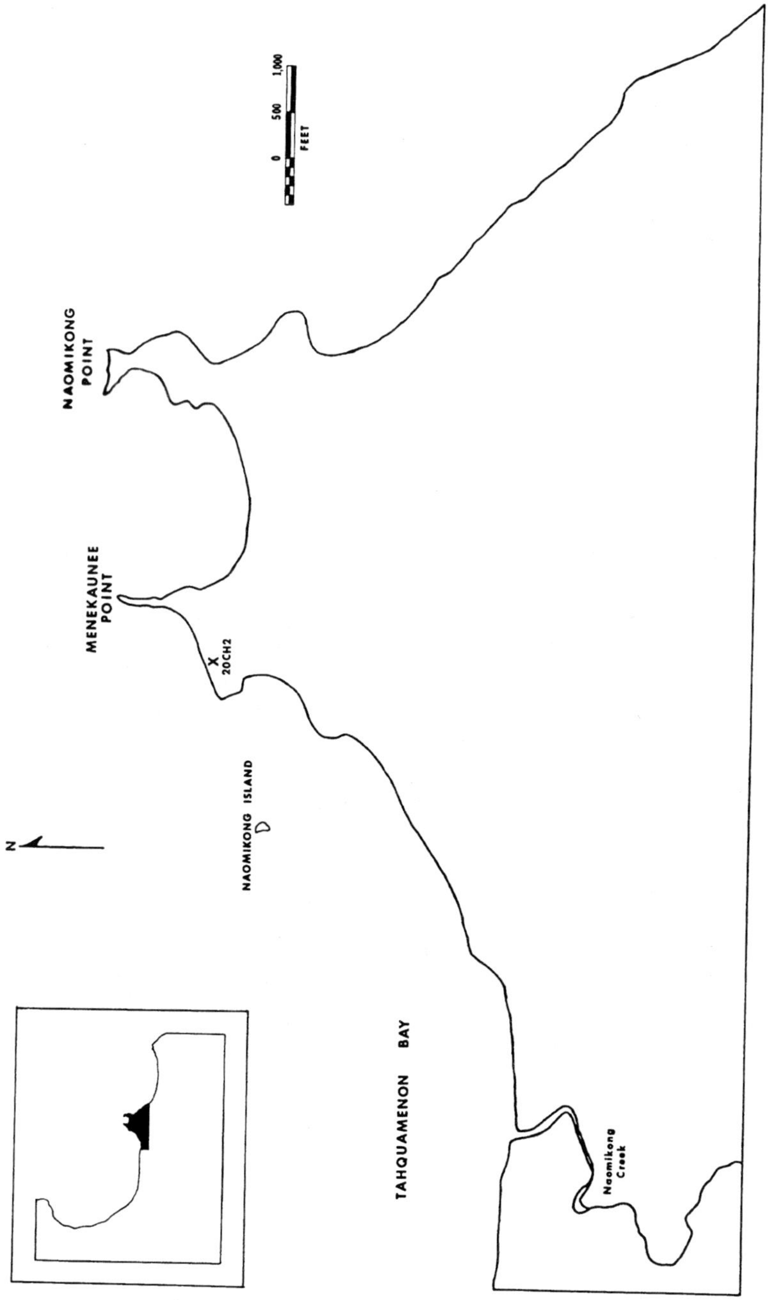

FIG. 2. Naomikong and Menekaunee Points.

individuals interested in the archaeology of the area. Equipped with wet suits and scuba gear, John Quimby and Mr. and Mrs. Thomas Fifield and their son George surveyed a section of the lake which had been laid out in a grid. A total of 264 sherds, and both historic and prehistoric artifacts were recovered in this operation (Quimby, 1965) (Fitting, n.d.).

Although no excavations could be conducted, the presence of twelve people participating in the survey meant a garbage pit and a latrine had to be dug in the meadow behind the beach. These two pits were dug with the utmost care, the profiles drawn, and all cultural material saved. The results of the survey were to reveal prehistoric material in the lake and in the latrine and garbage pit.

By August of the same year permission had been granted to the University of Michigan Museum of Anthropology to work on Naomikong Point. At this time, 120 miles to the southwest, the museum was conducting a survey and excavation at Burnt Bluff, Michigan, on the Garden Peninsula. Part of the Burnt Bluff crew, consisting of James E. Fitting, John Speth, Douglas Lugthart, and Richard Davis made a trip to Naomikong Point to put in a test trench. A 5- by 20-foot trench was opened in the meadow about 60 feet from the lake. A large quantity of sherds and flint chippage was recovered, as well as ground stone, copper, and flint artifacts. The presence of fire-cracked rock and trash pits verified that Naomikong Point was everything that Taylor had suspected, and was indeed a site worthy of extensive excavations.

Thanks to a National Science Foundation grant it was possible for the University of Michigan Museum of Anthropology to spend two field seasons at Naomikong Point. The 1965 survey had learned the hard way that in early June the area is infested with mosquitoes, and for this reason excavations were conducted in July and August. The 1966 season was directed by James E. Fitting and lasted from June 29 to July 26. The following year I directed a six week season from July 3 to August 12. Both seasons were successful and yielded large quantities of material. Before this material is discussed, the geology, flora, fauna, and geography of the area will be presented.

GEOLOGY

Lake Superior, the most northern of the Great Lakes, is the largest fresh water lake in acreage in the world, with a surface area of 31,820 square miles. Its greatest depth is 1,302 feet and its elevation varies from 601 to 602 feet above sea level. The lake lies almost entirely within the Canadian or Laurentian Shield, a large mass of Precambrian rocks which covers most of Canada east of the Great Plains. The geological history of the Great Lakes, as that of known bodies of water, is one of fluctuating glacial activity. Various periods of glacial advances and retreats have altered the sizes and shapes of the lakes, and changes in the drainage outlets have affected the lake levels through time. As a direct result of these activities the Lake Superior region remained uninhabitable during periods when man was spreading throughout North America.

Around 11,500 years ago the entire Superior Basin was filled by Valders ice. By 10,500 years ago the retreating ice had produced a series of glacial lakes in the Superior Basin, the largest being Lake Duluth. The various Duluth lake stages were about 225 to 150 feet above the present surface of Lake Superior (Hough, 1963:102). The latter part of the Lake Duluth stage corresponds with the Lake Algonquin stage in Lakes Michigan and Huron. According to Hough (1958:219-22) there is evidence indicating that the eastern part of the Superior Basin was still under glacial ice at this time and therefore Lake Algonquin never extended into this region. With continuing glacial retreat the Trent Valley outlet of Georgian Bay was uncovered allowing a discharge for Lake Algonquin. This resulted in a series of low-lake stages culminating in the Chippewa-Stanley stage in the Michigan and Huron Basins. A similar low stage is postulated for the Superior Basin, the Houghton stage, 340 feet above sea level, which drained over a sill at Sault Ste. Marie and discharged into Lake Stanley. Considering the rate of uplift between 10,500 and 9,500 B.P., the various lake stages that occurred during this period were quite short-lived. Sixteen to eighteen shorelines occur between the Lake Duluth and Houghton stages, and an estimate of 50 to 150 years for the duration of these stages has been made (Farrand, 1962:189).

Geological data for Post Algonquin times in the Superior Basin is sparse, and the exact events of several thousands of years are poorly known. Following the series of Post Algonquin low-lake stages, the uplift of land, resulting from the retreating glaciers, became the major factor in producing changes in the Upper Great Lakes. With the rise of the North Bay outlet, an increase in lake level in the Huron Basin and then in the Michigan Basin was produced. Hough (1963:104) has placed one step in this rise at 8,500 B.P. Eventually the rising lake reached the level of the old Lake Algonquin outlet beds, and the lakes began to discharge through the St. Clair River and Chicago outlets. As the North Bay outlet continued to rise, it closed, leaving only the two southern dischargeways. These series of events initiated the Nipissing stage, and by about 4,200 years ago it had risen to its highest level, 605 feet above sea level, the same as that of the maximum Algonquin stage. Unlike Lake Algonquin, the 605-foot Lake Nipissing extended into the Superior Basin because the sill at Sault Ste. Marie was submerged.

In the Michigan and Huron Basins, continued down-cutting of the St. Clair outlet allowed the lake level to be lowered to 595 feet, initiating the Algoma stage. Lake Algoma lasted until approximately 3,200 years ago, as indicated by a radiocarbon date for an Indian burial in the crest of an Algoma beach deposit at Saginaw, Michigan (Crane and Griffin, 1960), when additional down-cutting of the St. Clair outlet brought Lakes Huron and Michigan to their present level of 580 feet above sea level.

In the Superior Basin the Algoma water level was controlled at about 595 feet above sea level by the outlet at Port Huron. Since 3,200 B.P. the Port Huron outlet has been down-cut to 580 feet, its present level, while in the same period of time the Sault has risen from 577 feet to 602 feet above sea level. A plot of the rate of down-cutting at Port Huron, against the uplift curve for Sault Ste. Marie, gives an intersection of the curves at 2,200 B.P. (250 B.C.). This is the approximate date of separation of Lakes Superior and Huron (Farrand, 1962:187-89). A linear rate in the down-cutting at Port Huron was assumed in plotting the curve. If a nonlinear rate is used, a difference of about ±150 years could result, giving the time of separation of the lakes a range from 400 to 100 B.C.

The sill at Sault Ste. Marie has continued to rise so that today the lake level is approximately 602 feet above sea level. Since Naomikong Point and the Sault are only about 30 miles apart the degree of uplift in the two areas can be considered equal. This means that in the vicinity of Sault Ste. Marie, since 250 B.C., the lake has continued to rise, but the relative position of the lake with respect to the shoreline has remained the same. At Naomikong Point the Nipissing beach now stands at 650 feet above sea level and is inland approximately 2,000 feet from the lake in some places. The Algoma beach elevation is now at 620 feet above sea level, and its distance from the present shoreline is about 1,200 feet. Therefore, at no time since the Nipissing Lake stage has the shoreline of Lake Superior, in this region, been lower than it is today.

The concentration of prehistoric cultural material at Naomikong Point is found 30 to 60 feet from the lake, however, artifacts can be found on the modern beach. Farrand's work (1962) indicates that the present shoreline came into existence around 250 B.C., and the proximity of the site to the lake suggests that this date may set the limits for the earliest possible time of occupation. If there was a nonlinear rate in the down-cutting at the Port Huron outlet, a range from 400 to 100 B.C. might represent the earliest date for habitation in this area.

FLORA AND FAUNA

Since the natural environment provides the most forceful background for natural selection in plant and animal life, it is logical that the episodes of glacial advances and retreats in the Upper Great Lakes would produce changes in plant and animal populations. In reconstructing the flora and fauna of the Upper Great Lakes during the last 10,000 years, the preservation of data is the most limiting factor. By far the most frequent and well-preserved data are provided by fossil pollens. Since plants are often sensitive indicators of climate, a range of information can be obtained from pollen profiles. Moreover, if the type of plant cover is known, it is possible to determine the kinds of fauna that the area will support.

While fossil pollens have the potential of providing this kind of information, it is unfortunate that very little work has been done in the Lake Superior area. Cushing (1965:408-14) presents data from northern Minnesota, and Potzger (1946) from northern Michigan, which may reflect the general situation south of the Superior Basin. There is general agreement among nearly all pollen diagrams from southern Michigan, Wisconsin, and Minnesota that sediments corresponding to the retreating Wisconsin ice of 9,000 to 13,000 years ago have a dominance of spruce (*Picea*) pollen. The Weber Lake profile from northeastern Minnesota shows the presence of spruce at around 9,500 B.C., reaching a climax by 8,000 B.C. By 7,500 B.C. spruce and pine (*Pinus*) occur in about equal proportions; thereafter pine increases in frequency as spruce decreases. Birch (*Betula*) appeared around 6,500 B.C. but was secondary to pine, which reached a climax somewhere around 4,000 B.C. Pine continues to the present as the dominant vegetation with spruce reoccurring about 3,500 years ago.

To accept this scheme at face value is not recommended since a particular local condition could produce a flora that is not representative of the entire region. In general, the major theme, with minor variations, would probably apply to the northern Wisconsin and Michigan areas. The presence of oak (*Quercus*) and/or birch in the last 6,000 to 8,000 years in the pollen diagrams from four other Minnesota sites and a central Wisconsin site, add to the possibility that these were also present around the south shore of Lake Superior in the same general time period (Cushing, 1965:410-11).

While the pollen data reflecting the forest successions in Post-Wisconsin times can be generalized into broad periods, it is possible to attempt a more precise treatment when dealing with present day flora and fauna. Within a large geographical area there may be a fluctuation in the frequencies of specific types of flora and fauna and these may form a gradient through space. It is often useful to subdivide an area into smaller units in order to better examine the distribution of biota. The defining criteria for the establishment of such subareas are in terms of the frequency of certain flora, or fauna, or their association, which is considered diagnostic for the particular area. The establishment of the subarea is therefore a function of the defining criteria, and changes in criteria may generate new subareas. The boundary of transition from one subarea to another is usually difficult to establish, and since one merges gradually into another, the division is made in terms of an arbitrarily defined relative frequency difference for the defining criteria.

Dice (1943) has defined twenty-nine subareas for North America and has termed these "biotic provinces." According to Dice (1943:3),

> Each biotic province, . . . covers a considerable and continuous geographical area and is characterized by the occurrence of one or more important ecological associations that differ, at least in proportional area covered, from the associations of adjacent provinces. In general, biotic provinces are characterized also by peculiarities of vegetation type, ecological climax, flora, fauna, climate, physiography, and soil.

If this classification is used, all but a small area of the north shore of Lake Superior would lie within the Canadian biotic province (Fig. 3). Potzger (1946:213-50) has noted that the forest type of the Canadian biotic province may be the result of the modifying effects of the large masses of water in this area. He has therefore called this floral assemblage Lake Forest. The climax vegetation is hardwood forest with several types of

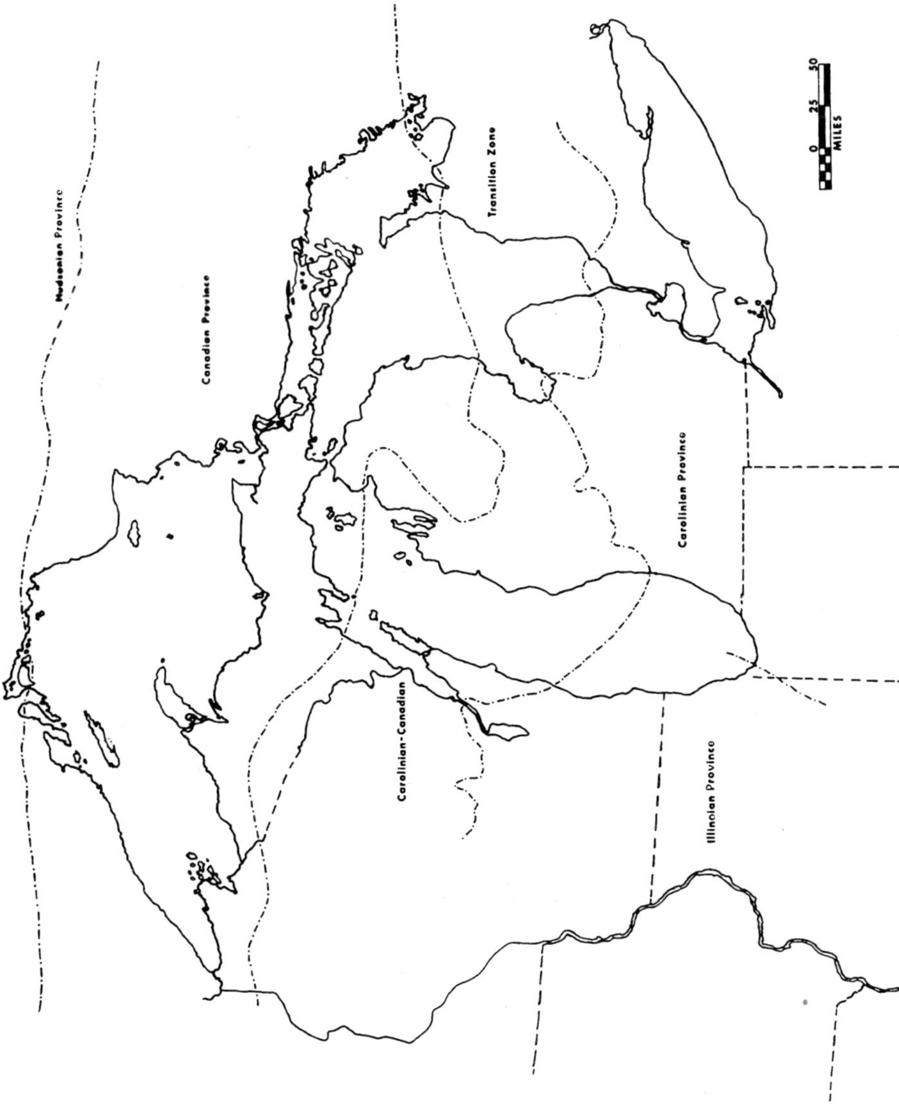

FIG. 3. Biotic Provinces of the Upper Great Lakes.

coniferous forest producing important subclimaxes. In general sugar maple, yellow birch, northern white pine, and eastern hemlock predominate. There may also be extensive stands of northern white pine and eastern hemlock with black spruce, tamarack, and northern white cedar occurring in bogs and poorly drained areas. Some portions of the Canadian biotic province represent recent changes in the flora and fauna and do not conform to the situation of a century or more ago. Schoolcraft's description of the Whitefish Bay area in the vicinity of the Tahquamenon River (Fig. 1) gives us the following information (Williams, 1953:103).

> In coasting along the shore for fifteen miles we passed the mouth of the Tahquamenon River, with a small island of the same name lying off its mouth, and proceeded three leagues beyond where we encamped at eleven o'clock at night, at the mouth of the Shelldrake River, having advanced a distance altogether of thirty-four miles. We generally kept within a mile of shore, and often much nearer so that it was constantly in plain sight. The shore of the lake thus far is sandy, without large pebbles, and with no bluff rocks at the water's edge. The growth of timber is pine, hemlock, oak, aspens, and birch.

Since Schoolcraft's visit in 1820, extensive lumbering activities in the last four decades of the nineteenth century have produced significant changes in the relative frequencies of the flora. Michigan pine played an important role in the building of Chicago and even more so in rebuilding the city after the fire of 1871. Lumbering in Michigan reached its production peak in 1890 when five and one-half billion board feet were cut. During the logging boom, and for some time afterwards, the drying debris which resulted from logging, provided tinder for the most devasting fires of the historic period. The net result of logging and fires was the destruction of the humus and organic composition of the soil. Gradually the burned areas were reforested but not with the original species. Only the hardy pioneer species; aspen, oak, and jack pine, were able to grow on the barren, sterile soils. The predominately pine forests which existed prior to lumbering were replaced by predominately aspen forests. Shelford (1963:138-39), partially quantifies the degree of change in forest cover that occurs after a forest fire by citing a study made in the Lake Nipigon area of Ontario. Prior to burning in about A.D. 1770, the area is reported to have been mostly pine forest. The composition of the late subclimax forest 175 years after the fire was: balsam fir, 59 percent; black spruce, 2 percent; white spruce, 10 percent; jack pine, 4 percent; and quaking aspen, 8 percent. These changes illustrate the degree of change that can take place. The possible repercussion on the fauna will be presented later.

As to the fauna of the Upper Great Lakes, animal populations probably moved into this region as soon as it was free of glacial ice. These species would have been living in the proximity of the glacier and would therefore have been those which tolerate cold conditions. The remains of a number of now extinct species, including American mastodon, giant moose, and giant beaver have been found in the Upper Great Lakes and date from 12,00 to 9,000 B.C. (Cleland, 1966:15). From an examination of the faunal lists of present-day mammals in spruce-fir environments, it is possible to infer that other faunal representatives occupying the region during the early post-glacial time might have included: caribou, black bear, fisher, marten, lynx, muskrat, and snowshoe hare (Burt and Grossenheider, 1964).

It is somewhat difficult to establish the history of the introduction of fish into the Great Lakes. In the Upper Great Lakes, as the glacial lakes grew, drainage connections with the upper Mississippi Valley and the Atlantic Coastal Plain were established and these formed the principal migration routes for fish. The routes by which the various species entered the Great Lakes is not well known, however, by the time man first entered this region all present-day species would have been represented (excluding those introduced in historic times), and their total number was no doubt larger than it is today.

With the establishment of the pine forest the fauna probably changed very little until the historic period. Certain of the large fauna such as mastodon, giant moose, and giant beaver became extinct and the latter two were replaced by modern forms. Caribou and musk-ox were also absent, having moved north with the retreating tundra. Aquatic birds such as gulls, loons, terns, mergansers, and various species of ducks were most likely on the lakes, and the spruce and ruffed grouse could be found in the coniferous forest. Even though the latter frequents hardwood forests most of the year it prefers coniferous woodlands during the winter (Edminster, 1947:74).

The most notable change in the fauna of the Upper Great Lakes occurred around the turn of the nineteenth century. White-tailed deer is not a coniferous forest species, however, after lumbering had cleared millions of acres of pine forest, the secondary growth was favorable for deer. Consequently deer is now found in the Upper Peninsula of Michigan and has succeeded in extending its range considerably. A previous boundary in central Wisconsin has been expanded about 500 miles north (Shelford, 1963:127).

GEOGRAPHY

The soils of Michigan's Upper Peninsula, the northern part of the Lower Peninsula, northern Wisconsin, and northern Minnesota, have been classified as true podzols. These soils are formed only when certain conditions involving temperature, rainfall, and vegetation are present. The presence of a type of organic matter which has the potential to develop acids and other substances of great solvent capacity is an essential requirement. In ideal situations a soil pH as low as 3.5 can be obtained while values of 4.0 to 4.5 are more common. Earthworms may be practically absent, and in general the soil has a relatively low agricultural value (Buckman and Brady, 1965:303-07). Particular local situations involving mineral content and drainage can effect the soil pH and produce slightly alkaline conditions (Whiteside, Schneider and Cook, 1964:66).

The discussion thus far has been general in its scope and relates to the entire Upper Great Lakes area and in particular to the Lake Superior region. At this point the emphasis will shift to the latter area with particular attention given to the southeastern portion. The topography of this region is rolling and is characterized by moraines, outwash plains, swamps, and rock outcrops. Numerous small streams with low, swampy, interstream areas are present, and the drainage pattern is irregular and haphazard in its development.

The climate of the southeastern portion of Lake Superior is characterized by yearly temperatures which fluctuate between a daily average high of 12 degrees Fahrenheit in January to a daily average high of 76 degrees Fahrenheit in July. The annual precipitation varies from 28 to 32 inches with an average of 31 inches. This includes approximately 100 inches of snow annually (Eichmeier, 1964:41-48). The length of the growing season ranges from 90 days in parts of the interior of Michigan's Upper Peninsula, to 150 days on portions of Lake Superior. The last spring freeze can occur from May 20 to June 10, while the first freezing temperature in the fall occurs from September 20 to October 1 (Hill and Mawby, 1964:181-82).

Recently Baerreis and Bryson (1965:203-20) have outlined a tentative series of climatic episodes for the time period from 500 B.C. to the present. It is possible that the data pertaining to climate, which have been presented for the southeastern portion of Lake Superior, will need revision when applied to prehistoric conditions.

PREHISTORIC PHYSICAL SETTING

From the information in the discussions on geology, flora, fauna, and geography of the Lake Superior region I will attempt to synthesize a picture of the physical setting at Naomikong Point during its prehistoric occupation. The site lies on the south shore of Tahquamenon Bay, a small bay in the southwestern portion of Whitefish Bay. The bay is defined by the Tahquamenon River to the north and Naomikong Point to the east. There is no evidence of occupation prior to Nipissing times and during the Nipissing and Algoma lake stages the site was submerged. Sometimes between 400 and 100 B.C. the shore of Tahquamenon Bay reached its present location and the area was open to habitation. The terrain was rolling with moraines, outwash plains, and rock outcrops. Numerous small streams and bogs were present and pine formed the dominant forest cover. Black spruce and northern white cedar grew in poorly drained areas while hemlock and aspen sporadically dotted the landscape. An occasional moose could be seen in a swampy area along the shore, while other mammals in the area included beaver, porcupine, muskrat, black bear, fisher, and marten. Fish and birds were probably more plentiful than mammals, and the waters of Whitefish Bay abounded with sturgeon, whitefish, lake trout, perch, and suckers. Birds included loons, terns, mergansers, and ducks, while inland grouse and passenger pigeon could be found.

The yearly temperatures were approximately the same as at present, as was the amount of precipitation. The winters were cold with snow on the ground from November to April. Migratory birds left the area during this time and Tahquamenon Bay froze.

II

UNIVERSITY OF MICHIGAN EXCAVATIONS AT THE NAOMIKONG POINT SITE

THE PROBLEM

ARCHAEOLOGISTS, in dealing with the remnants of prehistoric societies, observe four basic categories of data in their excavations. These are artifacts, non-artifacts, features, and associations. This is the data from which temporal, spatial, and cultural inferences are drawn.

The method of collection of this data and the manipulation of it in a laboratory is largely influenced by the philosophy of the archaeologist and the questions he is asking. The Naomikong Point excavations were conducted with certain questions in mind, and the data have been analyzed in terms of answering these questions.

Once the archaeologist has obtained his data the first problem is to identify the cultural affiliation, or affiliations of the site. At the Naomikong Point site the majority of the material could be classified as Laurel with a relatively small amount assignable to Late Woodland cultures. These identifications were not the result of long hours of analysis in the laboratory but could be made in the field as the material was being recovered. This was possible because the ceramic assemblage of each of these two groups is distinctive. The basis of this report will deal with an analysis of the Laurel material.

Laurel, originally defined by Wilford (1941) for a Middle Woodland manifestation in northern Minnesota, has now been extended to include parts of the provinces of Ontario, Manitoba, and Saskatchewan. Recently Mason (1967) called attention to a Laurel-like component on the Door Peninsula in Wisconsin, thus initiating this area into the Laurel family. Prior to work at Naomikong Point, the spatial distribution of Laurel sites excluded the south shore of Lake Superior, and this region was considered marginal to the major development whose focal point was to the north and west. The Naomikong Point site has not only yielded Laurel ceramics, but has done so in a quantity so far unmatched at any other site. One of its contributions has been to extend the southern limits of Laurel and thereby demonstrate a far greater range to this culture than once imagined.

The problems that will be considered in this report can be oriented around the three basic kinds of archaeological, interpretation; namely temporal, spatial, and cultural. These will be referred to as dimensions, and the goal is to examine the dimensions of Laurel. To date, most studies have concentrated on the temporal and spatial dimensions. The most noteworthy example is Wright's (1967) synthesis of Laurel in which he postulated four hypotheses as to its origin. The cultural dimension has been probed only in so far as artifact descriptions and comparisons are concerned. The only attempt to go beyond this is Stoltman's 1962 study where a modal analysis was performed on the pottery from five Minnesota Laurel sites. To extract "culture" from artifacts, non-artifacts, features, and associations requires that the data be collected and analyzed in a particular way. Even the interpretations are in terms of inferences which may have relatively low degrees of reliability. To be sure, many aspects of aboriginal life will escape the grasp of the archaeologist, but there are some which may be revealed. Hints as to group size, subsistence pattern, settlement pattern, and exploitation of natural resources may be derived from these data. These aspects of the cultural dimension are the problems to be investigated in this study.

In order to obtain data to examine these patterns large areas of the site were excavated. This allowed the spatial distribution of artifact classes to be defined, as well as the associations of fire and trash pits, chippage areas, and areas of habitation. The total site was divided into smaller units with the material from each unit kept separate. Product-moment correlation coefficients were then calculated for each of these units over the entire site for all pairs of artifactual and non-artifactual material. This type of analysis reveals highly correlated groups of material from which task-specific areas can be inferred.

This brief sketch of some of the techniques of excavation and analysis has been presented in order to clarify the problem and how it will be approached. Once all the archaeological data has been assembled it will be viewed from a particular frame of reference. This framework is the prehistoric ecological setting. It establishes the constraints and potentials of the area in terms of such factors as natural resources, flora, fauna, and possible habitation areas. Given these conditions, the problem is to determine how the environment was exploited by the Laurel culture as seen from Naomikong Point. Naomikong Point can be used as a model and this model can be tested against other Laurel sites as well as neighboring sites showing Laurel influences.

NATURE AND EXTENT OF EXCAVATIONS

The Naomikong Point site is designated as 20CH2, 20 referring to the state of Michigan, CH to Chippewa County, and 2 to the second site in Chippewa County recorded in the University of Michigan Museum of Anthropology site records. Figure 1 shows the location of Naomikong Point relative to other landmarks in the Whitefish Bay area. Figure 2 is a more detailed map of Naomikong Point and the location of the excavations is indicated. It will be noted that a discrepancy exists and that the Naomikong Point site is not situated on Naomikong Point. The entire region of Naomikong and Menekaunee Points is commonly referred to as Naomikong Point, and place names like Naomikong Creek and Naomikong Island indicate how widely this term is used. The name of the site also reflects the flexibility in the use of Naomikong Point to designate a precise location.

The site is located in a high grass meadow, inland about 30 feet from the lake with a forest-swamp bordering the meadow to the south. No artifactual material can be detected on the surface, and the location of the excavation was arbitrarily placed inland about 50 feet from the lake. Figure 4 shows a map of the site with the excavation units and indicates the 1965 test trench and the 1966 and 1967 excavations. A grid system was established with a datum point at 500 E 500 (north 500 feet, east 500 feet from some point defined as the zero point). A unit size of 20- by 20-feet was selected as sufficient for revealing any spatial differences reflecting social activity and this was excavated in 5- by 5-foot subunits. The latter were considered adequate for collecting a large quantitative sample which could demonstrate areas of specialized activity within the 20- by 20-foot unit. By excavating staggered, continguous units, the probability of securing this kind of information was increased. Each 20- by 20-foot unit was given a letter designation as shown in Fig. 4. The site was excavated in two distinct levels, surface-to-midden and midden. The rationale for excavating as a single unit will be discussed in the section on stratigraphy. In units A, B, and C, a 10- by 10-foot surface-to-midden unit was excavated, while 5- by 10-foot units were used for this level in units D and E, the 5 by 60, 5 by 30, and beach trenches. In

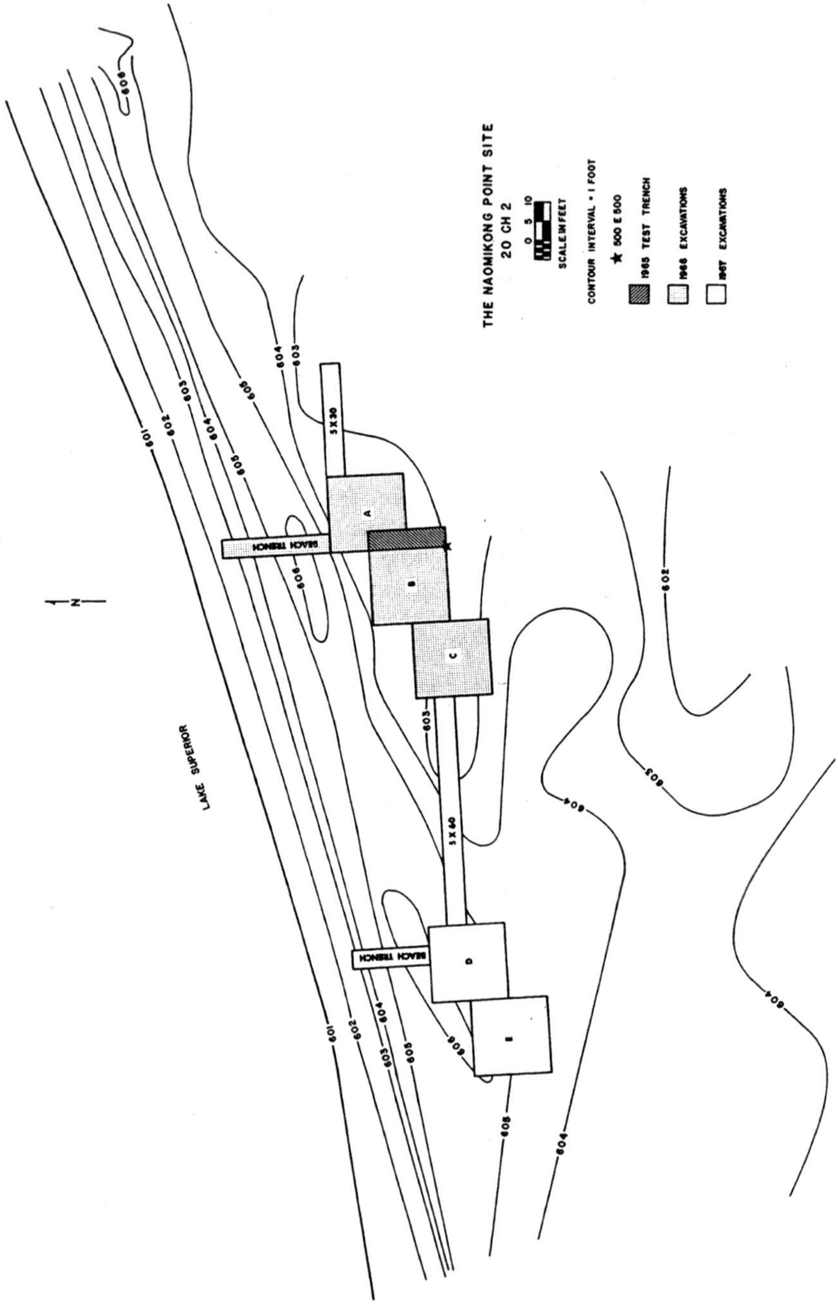
THE NAOMIKONG POINT SITE
20 CH 2
0 5 10
SCALE IN FEET
CONTOUR INTERVAL = 1 FOOT
500 E 500
1965 TEST TRENCH
1966 EXCAVATIONS
1967 EXCAVATIONS
LAKE SUPERIOR
BEACH TRENCH
5 X 30
5 X 60
A
B
C
D
E
N
601
602
603
604
605
606

FIG. 4

all cases the midden was excavated in 5- by 5-foot units. Each unit was designated by the location of its southwest corner in the grid system. Figure 5 shows a breakdown of the excavation into the 5- by 5-foot midden units and gives the designation of each unit.

In 1967 excavations were conducted 60 feet west of those in 1966 and a 5- by 60-foot trench connected the two major excavations. Beach trenches were dug both seasons in order to examine the nature of the dune formation. The 1967 crew extended a 5- by 30-foot trench eastward from unit C in hopes of defining the limits of the site. The results indicated that there was no reduction in the quantity of artifactual material and the midden was as productive as in unit C.

In two seasons a total of 2,750 square feet were excavated at the Naomikong Point site. This covered a distance of 190 feet east and west and represented 110 5- by 5-foot units.

The historic component at Naomikong will not be discussed in this report. A preliminary analysis has identified this occupation as historic Chippewa and dating around 1850. Dan Caister, a student at the University of Michigan and a member of the 1967 crew, has prepared a manuscript on the historic occupation and placed it on file at the University of Michigan Museum of Anthropology.

STRATIGRAPHY OF THE SITE

The nature of the stratigraphy varied from east to west and to a large extent was influenced by vegetation. Units A, B, C, the 5- by 30-foot trench, and 30 feet of the 5- by 60-foot trench, were shielded from the beach by small, dense, scrub vegetation. No blow sand had accumulated in this area because of the barrier afforded by the vegetation. In this protected area, directly beneath the sod zone, an historic midden was encountered which was usually two-tenths to five-tenths of a foot in depth and intruded into the prehistoric midden causing a mixing of material. Stratigraphically, a division of these middens could not be detected, and as shown in Plate II*a* the total cultural deposit in some areas was very shallow. Moving west, the vegetation inland from the beach had been removed and up to two feet of blow sand covered the midden. Plate II*b* illustrates the amount of windblown sand that had accumulated in the western half of the 5- by 60-foot trench and should be contrasted with Plate II*a* which shows a profile of the eastern part of the same trench. The former area must have been cleared at the time of the

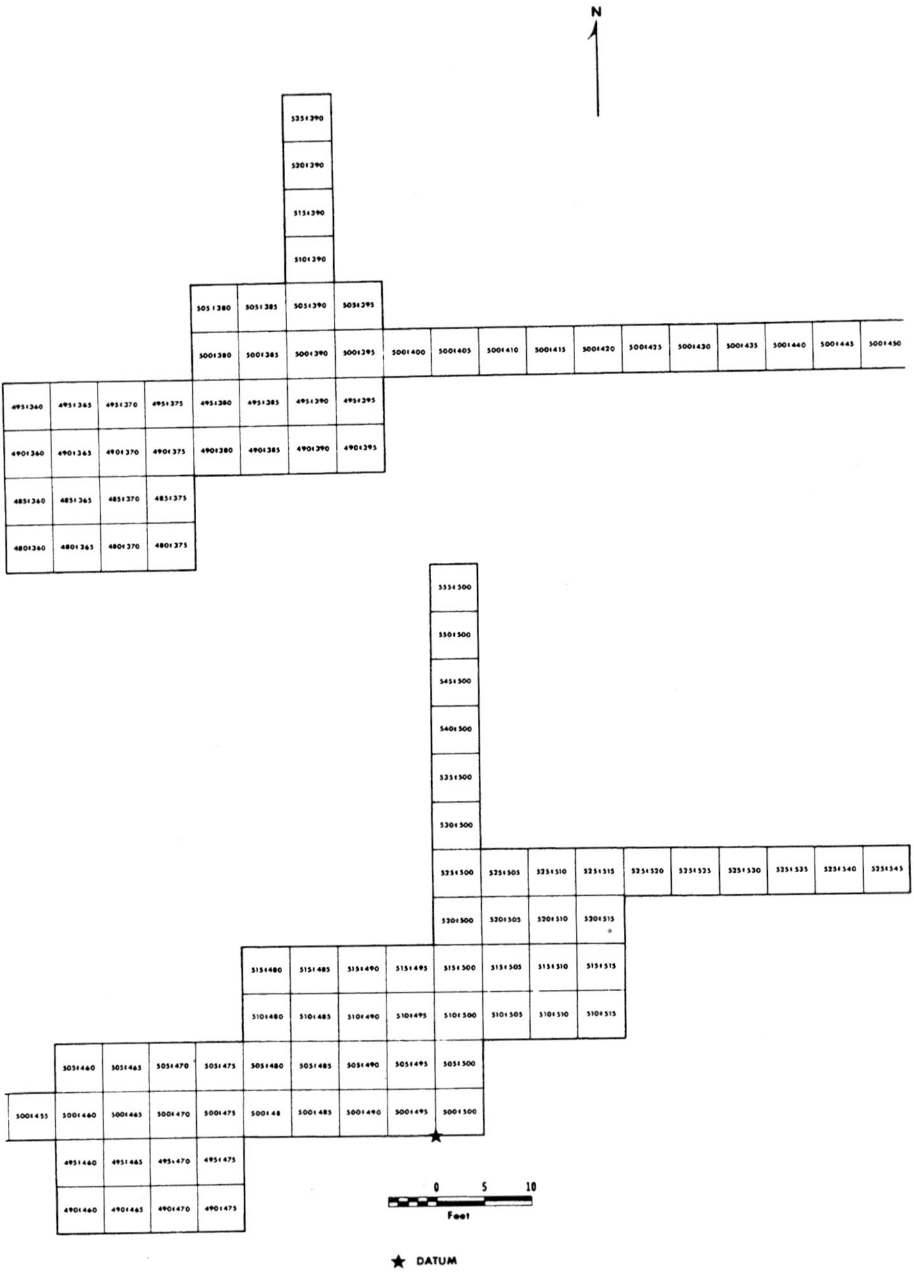

FIG. 5. Five- by five-foot unit designations for the Naomikong Point site.

mid eighteen hundred occupation since its cultural debris was directly above, and partially mixed with the prehistoric midden. The blow sand was almost totally sterile. Five- by ten-foot units were excavated in the surface to midden zone and these yielded only a few rocks. In one case several tin cans and broken bottles were found and this probably represented an occupation that occurred around 1900. Mr. Austin Johnson, now living in Oak Ridge, Tennessee, visited the site during the 1967 season and informed the crew that he had lived in the vicinity of the excavations in 1903. He reminisced on the living conditions at that time and related how string and cord were preserved with a coating of tar. The next day a fragment of tarred string was recovered from the dune sand in opening a 5- by 10-foot unit.

Since there was no apparent stratigraphic division between the historic and prehistoric middens, surface-to-midden levels were excavated to a depth where prehistoric artifacts first occurred. This point was used to define the start of the prehistoric midden. As the word "midden," in surface-to-midden is used it refers specifically to the prehistoric level. Because of the partial mixing of these two middens in some areas, the usefulness of charcoal samples from the prehistoric midden for carbon-14 dating is questionable. An attempt was made by the 1966 crew to excavate the prehistoric midden in two distinct levels, however, it was found that often sherd concentrations started at the top of the midden and continued to the bottom. Since the average depth of the midden ranged from two-tenths to seven-tenths feet, it was decided that the midden would be excavated as a single unit. The 1967 excavations verified these results and no instances of stratification, such as thin lenses of sterile sand separating distinct midden zones were encountered. In only one instance did a discontinuity in the midden occur, and this was in the 5- by 60-foot trench. At 500 E 440 a wedge of brown mottled sand cut into the prehistoric midden and within a distance of three feet (500 E 437), had completely separated the midden into two distinct zones. At 500 E 434 the midden stopped and did not reappear until 500 E 428. Figure 6 shows the south wall profile of the 5- by 60-foot trench with the midden discontinuity. A more detailed view is presented in Figure 7. The significance of this hiatus in the midden and its relevance to the interpretation of the archaeological evidence, will be discussed in detail in a later chapter.

It will be noted that the sidewall profiles shown in Figure 6 indicate areas where the midden attains a depth greater than two-tenths to seven-tenths of a foot, previously mentioned as the

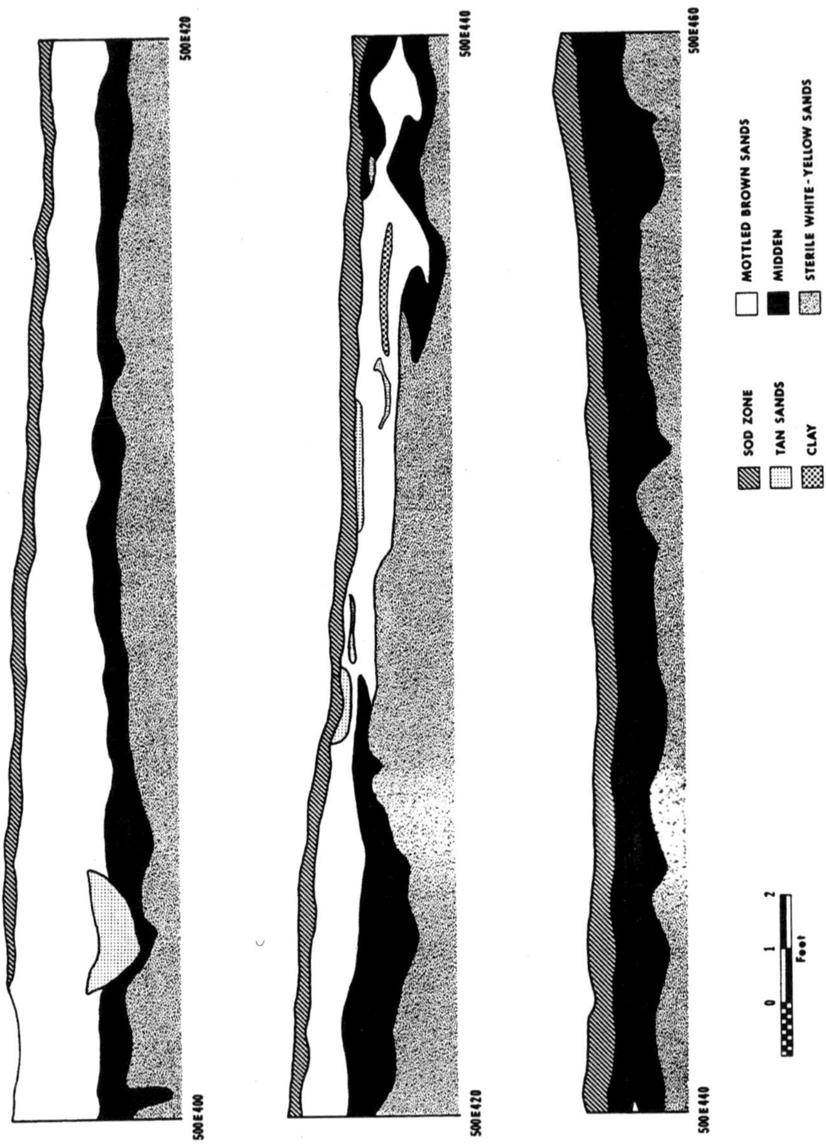

FIG. 6. South wall of 5- by 60-foot trench.

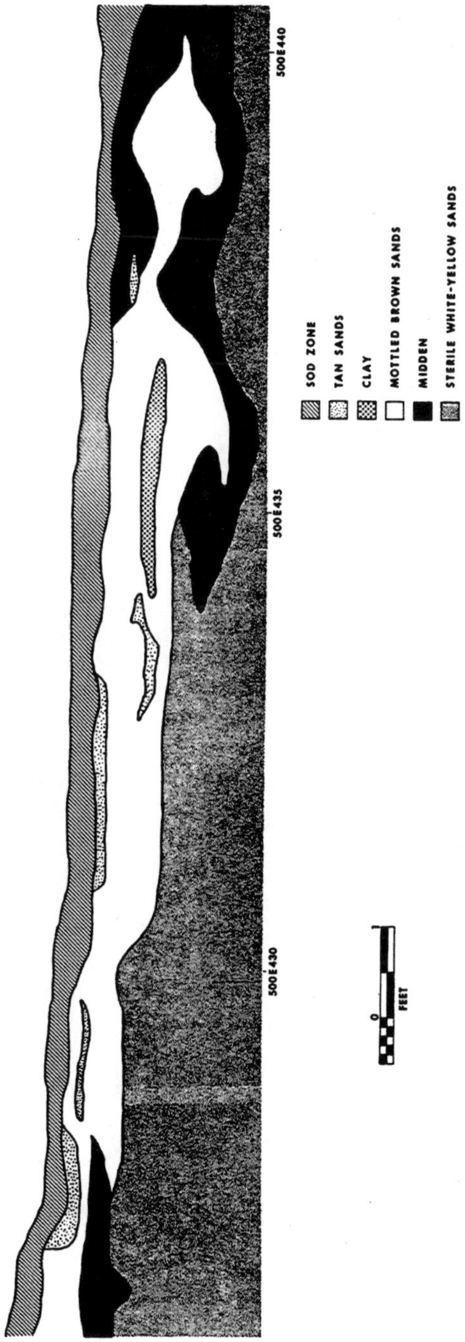

FIG. 7. Midden discontinuity in south wall profile of 5- by 60-foot trench.

average depth. These cases are either features or natural depressions in the midden, and are confined to a relatively small area.

Beneath the midden, sterile white-yellow sands were found. Several units were excavated below the midden and no lower levels of cultural deposits were present. In the northwest corner of unit E large water-worn cobbles were encountered at four and seven-tenths feet below ground level, and the water table occurred in another three-tenths of a foot. A profile of the northern half of the west wall of unit A and the west wall of the 1966 beach trench is shown in Figure 8. Munsell colors were used to define colors in all the profiles. The designation "tan" corresponds to "pale brown," and "white-yellow" to "white" and "very pale brown" in the Munsell system.

EXCAVATION TECHNIQUES

The excavation techniques can be described as those commonly practiced by "Great Lakes" archaeologists. Excavating equipment included long-handled, flat-nosed shovels, trowels, and dental-picks. All dirt was screened with one-quarter inch hardware cloth, and features and suspected features were troweled and fine-screened through either one-eighth inch hardware cloth or window screen. The rock from each excavated unit was weighed and in some instances counted. Material from features was bagged separately and the associated rock was weighed. An attempt was made to recover artifactual material *in situ* and to plot its location on the site map. With the tremendous quantity of material recovered it was impractical to record the location of each artifact, however when possible, projectile points, notched stones (net sinkers), copper artifacts, and copper fragments were plotted on the site map. Large concentrations of sherds and chippage were bagged separately, their location recorded, and labeled as "noted items." Post molds were sectioned and their location noted on the site map. A number of soil samples was collected and five vertical, linear series were taken.

The standard University of Michigan Museum of Anthropology square sheets and feature forms were used for recording information, and in addition a set of notes was kept for each unit. Drawings of floors and sidewall profiles were made on square sheets and Munsell colors were used for defining color differences. This record was duplicated with black and white and color photographs.

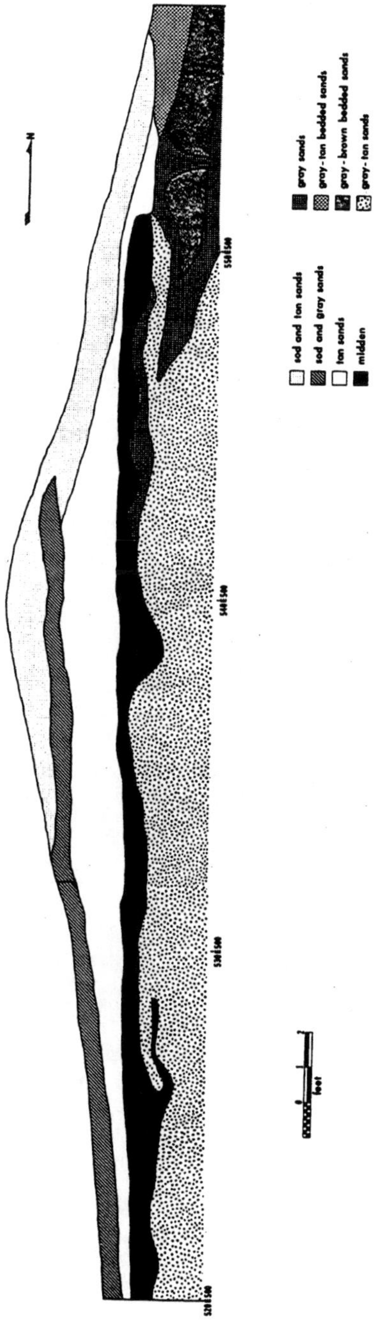

FIG. 8. West wall profile of unit A and 1966 beach trench.

FEATURES

During the excavations at Naomikong Point a total of 47 features were identified. By combining some of these into a single feature, and by rejecting others, this number was reduced to 38. The most frequent means of recognizing features was by a discoloration, or texture difference in the soil. The midden varied in color from brown to black and features were usually dark black and in some cases pink or dark brown. Rock arranged in a circular or semicircular pattern also served to define a feature. Concentrations of artifactual material, usually sherds, were not considered as features unless they could be delimited from the midden on the basis of soil color or texture. When not classified as features these concentrations were numbered and labeled as "noted items." Features were numbered starting with 1 and a suffix 65, 66, or 67, used to designate the features from the 1965, 1966, and 1967 excavations.

Two types of features were encountered; historic and prehistoric. Since the historic component rested on the prehistoric midden, it was often difficult to determine whether the feature was historic, intruding into the prehistoric midden; or prehistoric, disturbed by the historic occupation. If a feature contained a large amount of prehistoric material and only one or two historic items it was classified as prehistoric. When the reverse proportions were encountered the feature was classified as historic.

A total of 109 prehistoric post molds was encountered in the excavations with 23 others less clearly defined and therefore only suspected as post molds. Figure 9 shows the location of features, prehistoric post molds, and sherd concentrations. The distribution of these will be discussed after the analysis of the artifactual material has been presented. Features which have been rejected are not included in this figure.

Each of the features will now be described and their contents listed. A complete analysis would require two or three pages per feature and such a treatment has not been attempted, although an effort has been made to condense as much information as possible into a brief description and to anticipate the kinds of data that will be most useful to those who wish to make site comparisons. The following format has been used in the descriptions. After the feature number, the unit, or units, in which the feature occurred is given. This is followed by the designation (5 by 5) or (5 by 10) corresponding to the dimensions of the unit in feet. Next the vertical location is given; surface-to-midden, midden, or bottom of midden. The shape of the horizontal profile and the

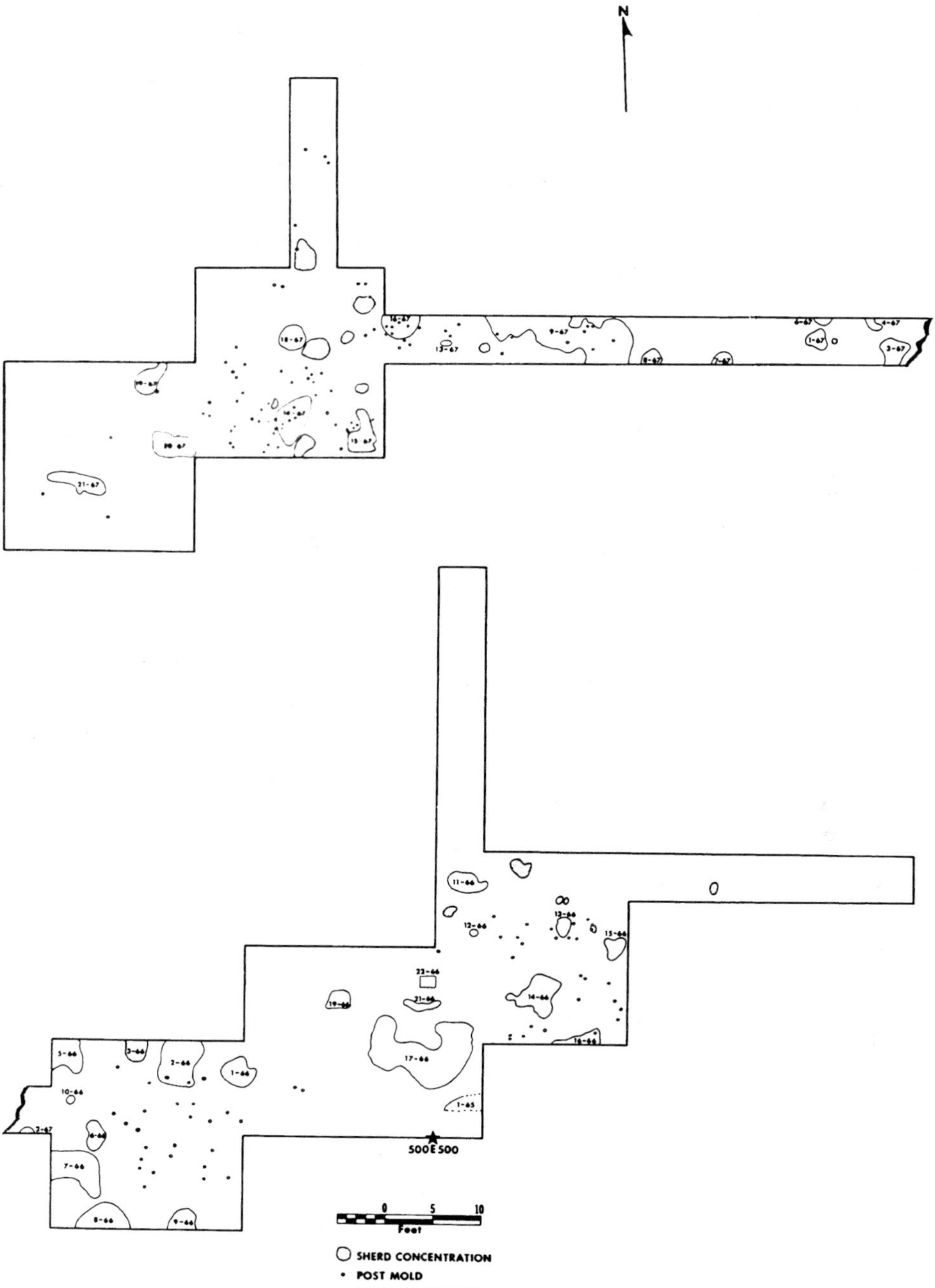

FIG. 9. Site Map showing the locations of features, post molds, and sherd concentrations.

maximum length, width, and depth is then given. Following this the contents are listed and their association to one another, referred to as association of elements, is presented. If the contents appear to be scattered haphazardly throughout the feature their association to one another is described as random. Next an interpretation of the feature is postulated, followed by a ceramic identification. The latter refers specifically to an identification of the decorative technique. Linear stamp indicates that the design was made with a plain tool, dentate refers to a notched tool, and pseudo-scallop shell to a particular type of dentate. The majority of the sherds were small and only those with a dimension greater than one inch were examined. Of these, one-half to three-fourths were plain and the type of decoration on many of the remaining sherds was obliterated. This situation accounts for the discrepancy between the number of sherds recovered and the number identified. In some cases, when a large number of sherds were present, an estimate of the number of vessels has been made.

Further mention should be made of the feature interpretations that are presented. The terms "refuse" and "storage" pit are tentative interpretations and are based on the dark black, greasy, nature of the soil. Fire pits are inferred from either a row of stones surrounding the feature or on the presence of pinkish sands which may indicate oxidation from heat. The function of a feature cannot be made with certainty, and in most cases an alternative interpretation can be proposed.

Feature 1-65: 500 E 500 (5 by 10), midden, semicircular, 2.0 ft. by 1.5 ft. by 10 ft. Contents: 15 sherds, 5 unmodified flakes, 5 lbs. fire-cracked rock. Association between elements is random. A large rock in the southern part of the feature limited excavating the entire feature. The feature is interpreted as a refuse pit. Sherds were too small for identification.

Feature 2-65: See Feature 17-66.

Feature 3-65: The feature was rejected.

Feature 4-65: See Feature 21-66.

Feature 5-65: The feature was rejected.

Feature 1-66: 505 E 475 (5 by 5) and 505 E 480 (5 by 5), midden, oval with straight sides and flat bottom, 4.0 ft. by 3.0 ft. by 1.0 ft. Contents: 30 sherds, 14 flint chips, 12 grams calcined bone, 209 lbs. fire-cracked rock. The western portion of the feature was difficult to define. Association of elements is random. The feature is interpreted as a fire pit based on the presence of pink sands bordering the feature. The sherds were too small for identification.

Feature 2-66: 505 E 470 (5 by 5) extending into 505 E 475 (5 by 5), midden, irregularly-shaped, 5 ft. by 4.5 ft. by 1 ft. Contents: 327 sherds, 5 scrapers, 6 utilized flakes, 1 core, 46 unmodified flakes, one bipointed copper object, 1 gram calcined bone, 21 lbs. fire-cracked rock. Association between elements is random. Two post molds were found under the feature. The feature is difficult to interpret and is probably a storage or refuse pit. Ceramic identification: 2 dentate-drag stamp sherds and 1 rim sherd with linear stamped decoration.

Feature 3-66: 505 E 465 (5 by 5) midden, oblong, 2.3 ft. by 2.4 ft. by 1.4 ft. Contents: 122 sherds, 5 scrapers, 3 utilized flakes, 12 lbs. fire-cracked rock. Association between elements is random. The feature is interpreted as a refuse or storage pit. Ceramic identification: 4 linear stamped sherds.

Feature 4-66: 505 E 465 (5 by 5), midden. After excavating this feature it was interpreted as a natural depression in the midden floor.

Feature 5-66: 505 E 460 (5 by 5), midden, irregularly-shaped, 3.5 ft. by 3.5 ft. by 0.5 ft. Contents: glass, 3 square nails, charred wood, pink daub, 359 sherds, 9 scrapers, 8 utilized flakes, 5 cores, 57 unmodified flakes, 3 notched stones, 1 hammerstone, 1 conical-shaped piece of copper, 0.5 grams calcined bone, 82 lbs. fire-cracked rock. The daub and charred bone were associated together and therefore the feature was interpreted as the remains of an historic dwelling. The large amount of prehistoric material may indicate that the structure had intruded into a prehistoric feature, but this could not be verified.

Feature 6-66: 500 E 460 (5 by 5) extending into 500 E 465 (5 by 5), 495 E 460 (5 by 5) and 495 E 465 (5 by 5), midden, oval, basin-shaped pit, 3.5 ft. by 2.4 ft. by 0.8 ft. Contents: 434 sherds, 77 flint chips, 13 grams calcined bone, 45 lbs. fire-cracked rock. Elements in feature are randomly associated. The southern half of the feature consisted of pink sands which may indicate oxidation by heat. The feature is interpreted as a fire pit. Ceramic identification: 5 sherds with pseudo-scallop shell decoration representing 1 or 2 vessels, and 1 rim sherd with linear stamped decoration.

Feature 7-66: 495 E 460 (5 by 5) extending into 490 E 460 (5 by 5), midden, irregularly-shaped, 5.0 ft. by 4.8 ft. by 0.8 ft. Contents: 493 sherds, 1 scraper, 2 utilized flakes, 8 unmodified flakes, 162 lbs. fire-cracked rock, fired clay, charred wood and bark, several pieces of glass, 2 square nails. The clay and historic material appear to be packed between two charred logs. The feature is interpreted as an open hearth in the center of what may be an historic cabin. The cabin may have rested on two logs and been packed with bark. This was placed on a naturally-occurring rock which actually represents the top of the prehistoric midden.

Feature 8-66: 490 E 360 and 490 E 365 (5 by 5), midden, semicircular (extends into sidewall), 5.9 ft. by 2.6 ft. by 0.7 ft. Contents: 479 sherds, 4 scrapers, 1 utilized flake, 2 cores, 5 unmodified flakes, several fragments calcined bone, 70 lbs. fire-cracked rock, scattered charcoal fragments. Association between elements is random. The feature is interpreted as a refuse or fire pit. Ceramic identification: 8 sherds pseudo-scallop shell decoration, 1 sherd with linear stamped decoration.

Feature 9-66: 490 E 470 (5 by 5) extending into 490 E 475 (5 by 5), midden, semicircular-shaped and extending into sidewall, 3.0 ft. by 2.6 ft. by 0.7 ft. Contents: 148 sherds, 4 scrapers, 1 core, 37 unmodified flakes, 6 grams calcined bone, 23 lbs. fire-cracked rock. Association between elements is random. The feature is interpreted as a refuse or storage pit. Ceramic identification: 3 body sherds pseudo-scallop shell decoration, 1 body sherd dentate decoration, 1 rim sherd linear stamped decoration.

Feature 10-66: 500 E 460 (5 by 5), midden, circular, 1.1 ft. by 1.0 ft. by 0.5 ft. Contents: 10 historic, clay pipe fragments, several nails and glass fragments, 1 fragment of unworked beaver bone, fish scales, 2 sherds, 2 unmodified flakes. Association between elements is random. The feature is considered historic but no further interpretation could be made.

Feature 11-66: 525 E 500 (5 by 5), midden, oval, 4.2 ft. by 2.4 ft. by 1.2 ft. Contents: 132 sherds, 14 unmodified flakes, 1 bipointed copper object, 1 net sinker, 80 lbs. fire-cracked rock. The copper object was resting on the net sinker and the fire-cracked rock was scattered throughout the feature. The feature was interpreted as a refuse or fire pit. Ceramic identification: 2 sherds with linear stamped decoration, 2 sherds with cord-wrapped paddle impressions.

Feature 12-66: 520 E 500 (5 by 5), midden, circular, 0.7 ft. by 0.7 ft. by 0.4 ft. Contents: charred wood and twigs. The bottom of the feature contained charred wood, topped with charred twigs. The wood was identified as conifer. This feature is not believed to be the result of animal activity and may represent a prehistoric smoke pit.

Feature 13-66: 520 E 510 (5 by 5), midden, oval, 2.1 ft. by 1.7 ft. by 0.4 ft. Contents: 51 sherds, 5 unmodified flakes, 1 lb. fire-cracked rock. All material was found in the first 0.2 ft. of the feature. Seven post molds formed a semicircle around the feature. The feature may have served as a smoke pit and the post molds as the frame for a drying rack. Ceramic identification: 2 sherds with dentate decoration.

Feature 14-66: 515 E 505 (5 by 5) and 515 E 510 (5 by 5), midden, irregularly-shaped, 4.7 ft. by 4.5 ft. by 0.5 ft. Contents: 582 sherds, 7 scrapers, 4 utilized flakes, 2 cores, 86 unmodified flakes, 3 grams calcined bone, 11 lbs. fire-cracked rock. Sherds were concentrated in the central part of the feature and fire-cracked rock in the southern part. The feature is interpreted as a refuse pit. Ceramic identification: 1 pseudo-scallop shell vessel consisting of at least 50 sherds, 5 sherds with linear dentate decoration, 7 linear incised sherds, 2 cord-marked sherds, 2 sherds Mackinac ware, 10 fabric-impressed sherds. The ceramics indicate that at least two time horizons are present. The situation seems to suggest that the feature was intruded by a later prehistoric occupation.

Feature 15-66: 520 E 515 (5 by 5) and 515 E 515 (5 by 5), midden, irregularly-shaped, 2.2 ft. by 2.0 ft. by 1.75 ft. Contents: 2 fire-cracked rock, scattered charcoal at the bottom of the feature. The feature consisted of an area of black sand and may represent a storage pit.

Feature 16-66: 510 E 510 and 510 E 515 (5 by 5), bottom of midden, irregularly-shaped, 5 ft. by 1.7 ft. by 1.7 ft. Contents: 79 sherds, 4 unmodified flakes, 4 small fire-cracked rock. A post mold is located in the eastern part of the feature. The feature is interpreted as a natural depression in the midden. The sherds were too small for identification.

Feature 17-66: 510 E 490 (5 by 5), 510 E 495 (5 by 5), 510 E 500 (5 by 5), 505 E 490 (5 by 5), 505 E 495 (5 by 5), 500 E 500 (5 by 10), midden, irregularly-shaped, 10.1 ft. by 5.0 ft. by 0.6 ft. This feature includes Feature 2 from the 1965 test pit and Feature 23-66. The latter was found to be an extension of Feature 17-66. Contents: 5330 sherds (338 decorated sherds with length greater than one inch), 36 scrapers, 43 utilized flakes, 39 cores, 386 unmodified flakes, 24 net sinkers, 1 hammerstone, less than 1 gram calcined bone, approximately 300 lbs. fire-cracked rock. There was a sherd concentration along the east wall of unit 505 E 495 (5 by 5), and a concentration of fire-cracked rock in the center of the same unit. The feature is interpreted as a refuse area. Ceramic interpretation: 4 to 5 vessels linear stamped decoration, 2 to 3 vessels linear stamped drag-stamp decoration, 2 to 3 vessels with horizontal rows of dentate tool-impressed decoration, 1 vessel with pseudo-scallop shell decoration.

Feature 18-66: Feature found to be a rodent burrow.

Feature 19-66: 510 E 485 (5 by 5) and 510 E 490 (5 by 5) extending into 515 E 485 (5 by 5) and 515 E 490 midden, rectangular, 2.0 ft. by 2.0 ft. by 0.3 ft. to 0.5 ft. Contents: 840 sherds, 8 scrapers, 3 utilized flakes, 2 cores, 22 unmodified flakes, 3 net sinkers, approximately 200 lbs. fire-cracked rock, charred wood. The fire-cracked rock was covered with a layer of clay and this is believed to be associated with historic material in the surface to midden level. The feature is interpreted as a historic hearth which intruded into the prehistoric midden.

Feature 20-66: Feature found to be a rodent burrow.

Feature 21-66: 510 E 495 (5 by 5) extending into 510 E 500 (5 by 10) where the feature was designated 4-65, midden, irregularly-shaped, 4.0 ft. by 0.7 ft. by 0.4 ft. Contents: 20 sherds, 1 utilized flake, 4 unmodified flakes, 3 small fire-cracked rock. The association of elements is random. The feature may be a natural depression in the midden.

Feature 22-66: 515 E 495 (5 by 5), midden, rectangular, 3.0 ft. by 2.0 ft. by 1.2 ft. The feature consists of a rectangular area of black sand with a yellow birch post imbedded in the center. The feature is an historic post.

Feature 23-66: This feature was incorporated with Feature 17-66.

Feature 1-67: 500 E 440 (5 by 10), surface to midden, irregularly-shaped, 2.3 ft. by 1.7 ft. by 0.5 ft. Contents: rusted metal, window glass, historic ceramics, 2 lbs. rock. Association between elements is random. Feature is interpreted as an historic refuse pit.

Feature 2-67: 500 E 455 (5 by 5), midden, oblong pit, 1.5 ft. by 0.7 ft. by 1.5 ft. Contents: 15 sherds, 3 unmodified flakes, 3 grams calcined bone, 11 pounds of fire-cracked rock. Association between elements is random. Feature is interpreted as a prehistoric refuse pit. The sherds were too small for identification.

Feature 3-67: 500 E 450 (5 by 5) extends into unit 500 E 455 (5 by 5), midden, oval pit, 3.2 ft. by 2.5 ft. by 1.1 ft. Contents: 357 sherds, 4 unmodified flakes, 150 lbs. of fire-cracked rock, 1 gram calcined bone, small amount of charcoal scattered throughout the feature. Associated with the feature were sherd concentrations, noted items 7, 8, and 10. The feature is interpreted as a prehistoric refuse pit or a fire pit. Ceramic identification: the sherds were very small and only 6 had a dimension greater than one inch. One plain vessel consisting of 3 sherds and 4 sherds with cord-wrapped paddle impressions was identified.

Feature 4-67: 500 E 450 (5 by 5) bottom of midden, oval pit, 1.6 ft. by 1.4 ft. by 0.5 ft. Contents: 315 sherds (all with maximum length less than one inch), 8 unmodified flakes, several small pieces of red ocher, daub. Association of elements: sherds appeared in a concentration, the daub occurred at the bottom of the feature. The feature is interpreted as a prehistoric trash pit. Sherds were too small for identification.

Feature 5-67: The feature was rejected and interpreted as a natural depression in the midden.

Feature 6-67: 500 E 445 (5 by 5) bottom of midden, irregularly-shaped, 2.0 ft. by 1.0 ft. by 0.6 ft. Contents: 94 sherds, 35 unmodified flakes, 1 unidentified copper object, 11 grams of calcined bone, scattered fragments of charcoal, several small pieces of red ocher. The association of these items is random. The bottom of the pit appears to have been lined with rock and a conical vessel bottom was found in this area. The feature is interpreted as a fire pit. Ceramic identification: 5 sherds with horizontal rows of linear stamped decoration.

Feature 7-67: 500 E 430 (5 by 5) bottom of midden, semicircular, 2.6 ft. by 1.5 ft. by 0.3 ft. Contents: 10 sherds, 10 flint chips, 2 scrapers, 2 utilized flakes, 15 lbs. fire-cracked rock. Association between elements is random. The feature is located at the east end of the midden discontinuity. The feature is interpreted as a refuse pit. Ceramic identification: one cord-wrapped-stick impressed sherd.

Feature 8-67: 500 E 425 (5 by 5) top of midden oval, 2 ft. by 1.3 ft. by 0.4 ft. Contents: glass, iron fragments, 1 flint chip, 1 net sinker. The historic and prehistoric artifacts are mixed and the feature appears to be a historic refuse pit protruding into prehistoric midden.

Feature 9-67: 500 E 425 (5 by 5), 500 E 420 (5 by 5), 500 E 415 (5 by 5), 500 E 410 (5 by 5), midden, irregularly-shaped, 15.1 ft. by 5.0 ft. by 1.1 ft. Feature 10-67, 11-67, and 12-67 have been incorporated into Feature 9-67. Contents: 1059 sherds (67 decorated), 1 corner-notched projectile point, 8 scrapers, 1 utilized flake, 42 unmodified flakes, 2 copper awls, 1 net sinker, 1 hammerstone, 237 lbs. fire-cracked rock, 4 grams calcined bone, small amount of charcoal scattered throughout parts of the feature. Six post molds occurred in the feature and in unit 500 E 415 (5 by 5) a semicircle of rock surrounded a sherd concentration. The feature is interpreted as a refuse area. Ceramic identification: in general the decorations were obliterated. All decoration was performed with an unnotched tool and consisted of rows of horizontal or vertical punctuations, or horizontal incisions.

Feature 13-67: 500 E 405 (5 by 5) midden, elliptically-shaped, 1.3 ft. by 1.0 ft. by 0.5 ft. Contents: 2 sherds, 1 white seed-bead, 2 grams of charred and uncharred bone, nails, scattered charcoal, and wood fragments. Charcoal, sherds, nails, and bone occur at the top of the feature, bead and wood fragments at the bottom. The feature is interpreted as a prehistoric pit with historic intrusion.

Feature 14-67: 490 E 385 (5 by 5) and 490 E 390 (5 by 5) top of midden, irregularly-shaped, 5.0 ft. by 3.5 ft. by 0.3 ft. Contents: historic ceramics, decayed wood fragments, nails, 3 sherds, 1 unmodified flake, scattered charcoal. The wood and nails occur together and 5 post molds occur in the feature. The feature appears to be part of an historic structure.

Feature 15-67: 490 E 395 (5 by 5) floor of midden, irregularly-shaped, 4.5 ft. by 3.0 ft. by 0.5 ft. Contents: 105 sherds, 15 scrapers, 4 utilized flakes, 2 cores, 80 unmodified flakes, 2 net sinkers, 1 hammerstone, 3 problematic ground stone artifacts, 4 small pieces of copper, less than 0.5 grams of calcined bone, 52 lbs. fire-cracked rock, scattered charcoal. The charcoal occurred at the bottom of feature. The feature is interpreted as a refuse pit. Ceramic identification: 3 sherds with horizontal rows of linear stamped decoration, 1 sherd with horizontal incisions.

Feature 16-67: 500 E 500 (5 by 5) bottom of middle, circular. The feature consists of an area of red sands. No artifactual material was associated with the feature. Six post molds occur in the midden above the feature but do not intrude into it. The feature is interpreted as a fire pit.

Feature 17-67: The feature assigned this number was rejected as a feature.

Feature 18-67: 500 E 390 (5 by 5) and 505 E 390 (5 by 5) midden, circular, 3.3 ft. by 3.0 ft. by 1.3 ft. Contents: 679 sherds (30 decorated), 1 preform, 20 scrapers, 2 utilized flakes, 153 unmodified flakes, 1 net sinker, 2 bipointed copper objects, 4 pieces of unworked copper, historic ceramics, shoe fragment, 26 grams calcined bone, 9 lbs. fire-cracked rock. The historic material was found at the top of the feature while fire-cracked rock and bone was concentrated at the bottom. The feature is interpreted as a prehistoric refuse pit with historic intrusions. Ceramic identification: decoration is almost obliterated, 8 sherds with horizontal rows of linear stamping, 2 sherds with horizontal rows of incised lines, 1 sherd with horizontal rows of twisted cord-impressed decoration, 3 sherds with cross-hatched incisions, 9 cord-wrapped-paddle impressed sherds.

Feature 19-67: 495 E 375 (5 by 5) midden, irregularly-shaped, 3.5 ft. by 2.0 ft. by 1.5 ft. Contents: 104 potsherds, 1 projectile point, 1 unmodified flake, 16 lbs. fire-cracked rock. Sherds occurred in a concentration. The feature is interpreted as a refuse area or fire pit. Ceramic identification: 26 sherds representing 1 vessel with horizontal rows of linear stamping with drag-stamp application.

Feature 20-67: 490 E 375 (5 by 5) midden, irregularly-shaped, 4.5 ft. by 2.5 ft. by 0.6 ft. Contents: 43 sherds, 5 scrapers, 5 utilized flakes, 2 cores, 18 unmodified flakes, 1 net sinker, 1 gram calcined bone, 91 lbs. fire-cracked rock, 1 historic clay pipe fragment. A human skull without mandible was found resting on sands directly north of the feature. No pit around the skull could be determined. The feature is an anomaly and no interpretation will be attempted. Ceramic identification: 1 sherd, horizontal rows of drag stamp, dentate decoration, 1 sherd with cord-wrapped-paddle impressions.

Feature 31-67: 485 E 365 (5 by 5) midden, irregularly-shaped, 6.0 ft. by 2.0 ft. by 1.2 ft. Contents: 67 sherds, 1 scraper, 4 cores, 97 unmodified flakes, 1 prehistoric clay pipe bowl (Plate XV*a*, *b*). The feature is interpreted as refuse pit. Ceramic identification: 16 sherds cord-wrapped-paddle impressions.

THE COLLECTION

The entire collection from the Naomikong Point excavations is presently stored in the Great Lakes Range of the University of Michigan Museum of Anthropology. Material from the 1965 test excavations is catalogued from numbers 70501 to 70548. The 1966 excavation is catalogued from 72601 to 73160 and 73601 to 73633 and the 1967 excavation from 76001 to 76552. Square sheets, feature sheets, and field notes are filed in the Museum of Anthropology, along with Data Analysis Forms for pottery, flint artifacts, and chippage, ground stone, copper, and faunal remains. Photographs and 35 mm. slides have been entered into the museum's permanent photographic collection.

III

DESCRIPTION OF ARCHAEOLOGICAL MATERIAL

POTTERY

Introduction

POTTERY provides the archaeologist with one of his most valuable categories of data. Since it is quantifiable, often frequent, and can reflect temporal, spatial, and cultural differences, when present, it has formed the backbone of interpretation. The pottery from the Naomikong Point site is no exception. It was the most frequent artifact, and over 133,000 sherds were recovered.

In the upper part of the prehistoric midden a few cord-marked sherds were recovered. These sherds were not part of the Middle Woodland component since cord-marking is not a characteristic of Laurel ceramics. All cord-marked sherds could be classified as Late Woodland and were compatible with McPherron's Juntunen ceramic typology (1967). The Late Woodland ceramics will be discussed later.

Since the identification of a Laurel component at Naomikong Point hinges on the pottery, special attention will be given to this category of data. The initial problem which must be faced is one of communication. The language of ceramic description is one of many dialects. Terms like "stab and drag," "push-pull," and "drag stamp" can all be translated as referring to a particular method of applying decoration. Among archaeologists there is some variation in the use of the terms bossing, punctates, internal punctates, and external punctates. There are also several different approaches to ceramic classification. Wright (1967) has approached a study of Laurel pottery from the point of view of attribute analysis, and has not attempted to cluster attributes into types. Stoltman (1962), Mason (1967), and others have followed the more traditional line and have established ceramic types. An attempt has been made to present the ceramic data from Naomikong Point so it will be useful to archaeologists operating in either frame of reference. A description of the ceramics will be presented so that both an attribute and a typological analysis can be extracted. Existing types will be applied whenever possible, and only when there is a deviation from several attributes will a new type be proposed. Hopefully this presentation will have some utility for those dealing with either attributes or types and will facilitate intraregional comparisons.

With these ideas in mind, a discussion of the procedure followed in analyzing the Naomikong Point ceramics will now be presented. Since all dirt was screened through one-quarter inch hardware cloth, a large number of very small sherds are represented in the total assemblage of 133,892 sherds. The collection was therefore divided into two categories, the criteria for separation being sherd size. An arbitrary length of one inch was selected as the cut-off point and only those sherds exceeding this length were used in the analysis. The remaining sherds were considered too fragmentary to serve as a valid sample for attribute analysis or typing, and instead were counted and weighed. The sherds over one inch were separated into three groups; plain, decorated without cord-markings, and cord-marked sherds, with and and without decoration. The latter category was distinctive and could be assigned to the Mackinac wares as defined by McPherron (1967).

The remaining two groups of sherds constituted the sample for the Middle Woodland analysis. Rim sherds and conical vessel bottoms were the main contribution of the plain sherds. The initial step in analyzing the decorated sherds was to establish subgroupings on the basis of the type of tool used to execute the decoration. Aside from seventeen sherds with fabric impressions, two basic tool types were delineated. These were an unnotched, or simple tool, and a notched, or dentate tool. Design elements produced with the unnotched tool were referred to as either linear stamps or punctates, whereas those made with a notched tool were called dentates. Three kinds of dentate tool decoration were recognized and a description of each will be presented later. Incising was considered a distinctive decorative type and placed in a category by itself. Tables 1 and 2 present the data that has been discussed thus far. The northern half of the test trench is included in unit A and the southern half with unit B.

Rather than concentrating on the sherd as the smallest unit for analysis, the vessel was regarded as a more valid unit. In order to determine the minimum number of vessels represented in the collection, rim sherds were examined. These were considered the most reliable indicators for defining vessels. To aid in establishing the total number of vessels, over 200 hours were

TABLE 1

TOTAL SHERDS WITH A DIMENSION OF ONE INCH OR GREATER

	Sherds	Frequency	Percent
Undecorated	Plain	13,391	17.63
	Cord-marked	928	4.89
	Linear stamped	1,508	7.95
	Small tool dentate	1,102	5.81
	Pseudo-scallop Shell	704	3.71
	Incised	298	1.57
Decorated	Cord decoration	161	0.86
	Fabric impressed	17	0.09
	Dentate stamped	16	0.08
	Combined techniques	9	0.05
	Unidentifiable	826	4.36
	Total	18,960	100.00

devoted to ceramic reconstruction. This resulted not only in a dozen or more partially complete vessels but also indicated the variation in vessel shape, size, and decorative pattern. A large number of both body and rim sherds were badly weathered and it was often impossible to determine the types of decoration. Plasticine impressions were used to verify identifications, however, even this technique proved inadequate for many cases. Table 3 gives a breakdown, by decorative type, of the body sherds not reconstructed into vessels. This data is presented for each of

TABLE 2

TOTAL SHERDS WITH A DIMENSION LESS THAN ONE INCH

Unit	Frequency	Weight (In Kilograms)
5 by 30	11,140	8.0
Unit A	25,446	18.9
Unit B	30,346	21.7
Unit C	13,127	10.8
1966 Beach Trench	1,287	1.1
5 by 60	8,207	7.4
Unit D	21,805	17.4
Unit E	3,126	3.2
1967 Beach Trench	448	0.4
Total	114,932	88.9

TABLE 3

DECORATED BODY SHERD FREQUENCY AND DISTRIBUTION

	5 by 30		Unit C		Unit B		Unit A		1966 Beach Trench	
	Frequency	Percent	Frequency	Percent	Frequency	Percent	Frequency	Percent	Frequency	Percent
Pseudo-scallop Shell	35	15.1	107	23.0	147	15.1	90	9.7	33	36.7
Small tool dentate	67	28.9	152	32.7	275	28.1	314	33.8	20	22.2
Linear stamped	28	12.1	105	22.6	295	30.2	340	36.6	21	23.3
Incised	21	9.0	10	2.2	57	5.8	45	4.9	3	3.4
Cord decorated	3	1.3	0	0.0	4	0.4	0	0.0	1	1.1
Fabric impressed	0	0.0	0	0.0	1	0.1	8	0.9	0	0.0
Combined techniques	0	0.0	3	0.6	1	0.1	0	0.0	1	1.1
Unidentifiable	78	33.6	88	18.9	197	20.2	131	14.1	11	12.2
Total	232		465		977		928		90	
	5 by 60		Unit D		Unit E		1967 Beach Trench		Total	
	Frequency	Percent	Frequency	Percent	Frequency	Percent	Frequency	Percent	Frequency	Percent
Pseudo-scallop Shell	66	15.4	28	4.1	19	8.4	19	17.6	544	13.1
Small tool dentate	86	20.1	60	8.8	9	4.0	22	20.4	1005	24.3
Linear stamped	183	42.8	306	44.9	60	26.4	22	20.4	1360	32.9
Incised	26	6.1	121	17.7	10	4.4	4	3.7	297	7.2
Cord decorated	2	0.5	22	3.2	46	20.3	0	0.0	78	1.9
Fabric impressed	0	0.0	4	0.6	4	1.8	0	0.0	17	0.4
Combined techniques	1	0.4	2	0.3	1	0.4	0	0.0	9	0.2
Unidentifiable	63	14.7	139	20.4	78	34.3	41	37.9	826	20.0
Total	427		682		227		108		4136	

the major excavation units so that the distribution over the site can be observed.

Having determined the minimum number of vessels for each decorative type, the next step was to examine how the decoration had been applied. At least three different kinds of dentate decoration could be recognized. One particular kind of dentate has been termed pseudo-scallop shell, a distinctive type for Minnesota and northern Ontario Laurel sites. The design consists of a sinusoidal motif and is produced by a tool which has alternate notching. A second type of dentate is dentate stamping. This results from vertically applying a notched tool to the vessel so several elements are produced by a single operation. The third type of dentate was referred to as "small tool dentate" in Table 1. Later, with further explanation, this decoration will be classified as a variety of pseudo-scallop shell decoration.

The procedure which was followed in the ceramic analysis was to consider what has been termed "decoration type" as the major attribute. For the preliminary analysis this attribute superseded all other attributes. Such a scheme follows the standard approach for defining Laurel types. The presence of secondary attributes such as circular punctates encircling the rim, interior decoration, or rim profile are not considered sufficient for defining a different type. Following this convention, the attribute of drag stamping, sometimes referred to as push-pull, or stab and drag, was not by itself considered a justifiable attribute for defining a new type. Drag stamping is a particular method of applying decoration. It consists of inserting the tool into the clay, pulling it out without leaving the surface, that is, dragging the tool along the clay, and then repeating the operation. Since this technique can be performed with either a dentate or a simple tool it crosscuts the major defining attribute. Therefore drag stamping was treated as a secondary attribute, and grouped with dentate sherds if the drag stamping was executed with a notched tool, and with linear stamped sherds if a simple tool was used.

The approach taken here is not that followed by other archaeologists. Stoltman (1962) has used the drag stamp attribute to define the type Laurel Push-and-Pull. Wright (1967) weighs the attribute of drag stamping equal to those of pseudo-scallop shell, dentate stamping and linear stamping. Mason (1967), however, recognizes that drag stamping can be performed with two kinds of tools and differentiates Simple Stab-and-drag (unnotched tool) from Complex Stab-and-drag (dentate tool). These practices are not without merit, particularly if it could be demonstrated that drag stamping has temporal or spatial significance within the Laurel tradition. The attitude reflected in this particular analysis is one of personal preference, and drag stamping is considered a secondary attribute. Since not all archaeologists share this viewpoint, the data on drag stamping will be presented so it can be extracted from the analysis and thus be compatible with other investigations.

To review the procedure thus far, decorated sherds with a length greater than one inch were separated on the basis of the type of tool used to execute the decoration. The minimum number of vessels represented in each sample was determined by examining rim sherds. Each group was then subdivided into smaller categories if variations could be detected in the tool type used to execute the decoration. Three classes of notched tool decoration were found, pseudo-scallop shell, dentate stamping, and small tool dentate. All three types of notched tools could be used to perform a drag stamp decoration. Unnotched tool decoration was considered as a single class and was not subdivided into smaller groups. In this case the decoration appeared to be the result of applying one design element at a time, an operation referred to as linear stamping. Evidence of using an unnotched tool in a drag stamp operation was present. Decoration by incising was treated in the same way as unnotched tool decoration and was not split into smaller groups. Similarly, plain vessels were considered as a single class, even those examples which had bossed decorations.

The ceramic classes which were established by this procedure, in general, correspond to the existing pottery types which Stoltman (1962) defined for Laurel. These names will be applied to the Naomikong Point ceramics when possible. In cases where there are differences in several secondary attributes the term "Naomikong Point variety" will be attached to the recognized type name.

Before turning to the discussion of the attributes considered in the analysis, these remarks should be prefaced with an observation derived from the Naomikong Point ceramic assemblage. Not only must an analysis deal with the various idiosyncrasies of archaeologists in classifying pottery, but also with the idiosyncrasies of the potter. This does not mean the way in which an individual made pots, but the degree of variation found in one pot. Fortunately the Naomikong Point ceramics provided some partially reconstructable vessels. Sherd versus vessel examination was enlightening. Some vessels displayed not only variation in lip, rim, and body thickness, but in one case the rim profile changed from outsloping to straight. Likewise a constant decorative motif was not always observed. One partially complete Laurel vessel with an outsloping rim and a diameter of 18 centimeters, was decorated with 12 parallel rows of a dentate tool-impressed design. The dimensions of an element were about 1 centimeter in length by one-tenth centimeter wide. Each row consisted of approximately 276 elements applied with a drag stamp method. The vessel was composed of an estimated 3,312 elements. To maintain a constant pressure and angle to the tool in applying this many elements would take an accomplished potter. This particular vessel showed a high degree of uniformity in the execution of the design, however, other vessels indicated that not all potters had achieved this degree of skill. In order to obtain a pseudo-scallop shell design the tool must be applied to the clay at a right angle. As this angle becomes more and more acute there is a transition from a pseudo-scallop shell decoration to a dentate stamp pattern. This change was verified by making impressions in plasticine with an alternate notched stick and varying the angle of incidence. A similar change from pseudo-scallop shell to dentate stamping was observed on a partially complete vessel from Naomikong Point. Some sherds showed a predominance of dentate stamping while on others the transition to a pseudo-scallop shell design could be seen. This illustrates that basing a typology or attribute analysis on small sherds could be deceiving, and a distorted picture might be generated.

This introduces another essential area of discussion. The most important single prerequisite of an attribute is that it can be defined objectively. In dealing with unnotched, or simple tool decoration, there is little difficulty in defining the tool type objectively. The notched, or dentate tool, presents a different situation. Three classes of notched tool decoration have been mentioned in conjunction with the Naomikong Point ceramic assemblage, pseudo-scallop shell and dentate stamping are two of these. The third requires some explanation since its validity is tenuous, and since it is objectively difficult to define. Unlike pseudo-scallop shell and dentate-stamped decoration, this type of motif is almost always produced in small elements measuring approximately one centimeter in length by one-tenth of a centimeter in width. The small size of the element makes identification of the tool difficult. The decoration is reminiscent of pseudo-scallop shell, however, small pseudo-scallop shell elements found on several vessels do not conform with this type of dentate. Plasticine impressions and microscopic examinations were conducted, but the results only confirmed that a notched tool was responsible for the decoration without revealing the nature of the implement. Various archaeologists familiar with Laurel ceramics have examined Naomikong Point sherds with this type of decoration and have offered opinions as to its classification. Some have suggested that the end of a frayed stick might be responsible for this design while others classify it within the category of pseudo-scallop shell. There has been some disagreement on the latter identification, demonstrating that even for a supposedly well-defined motif like pseudo-scallop shell there is a range in opinion as to what constitutes this decoration. Since decoration can be a function of how the tool is applied to the clay, several attempts were made to duplicate the design with a small pseudo-scallop shell tool. Comparison of the results was encouraging. The closest match was obtained by applying a pseudo-scallop shell tool obliquely into the plasticine. Such a technique will produce dentate stamping if only a small amount of pressure is applied, and a different motif is generated by applying more pressure to the implement. The latter seemed to best duplicate the type of dentate being investigated, however not all vessels conformed and a few cases of uncertainty existed. Figure 10 illustrates the multiplicity of decorative motifs that can be obtained from dentate tools by varying the angle of application. The situation reiterates the remarks made in an earlier discussion where two different design elements appeared on the same vessel. In that case the difference was interpreted as accidental, while in the case at hand the decoration seems to be overt. The vessels examined do not show a transition from perpendicular to obliquely applied pseudo-scallop shell and therefore it is concluded that this may reflect a distinctive decoration. What we are dealing with is a continuous spectrum of design elements, each being a product of the angle and pressure on the tool. To divide such an assemblage into types is analogous to assigning names in phyletic speciation. The extremes can be objectively defined but the transition zones require subjective decisions. MacNeish (1958:148-51) has attempted to deal with this problem and has defined the type Nutimik Oblique for decoration composed of closely-spaced oblique pseudo-scallop shell-like impressions. Unfortunately illustrations of this type seem to include proper Pseudo-scallop shell sherds. Perhaps the best solution is to lump all dentate decoration into one category; but this may obliterate sensitive temporal, spatial, or cultural indicators. Therefore, rather than conceal a potentially significant attribute,

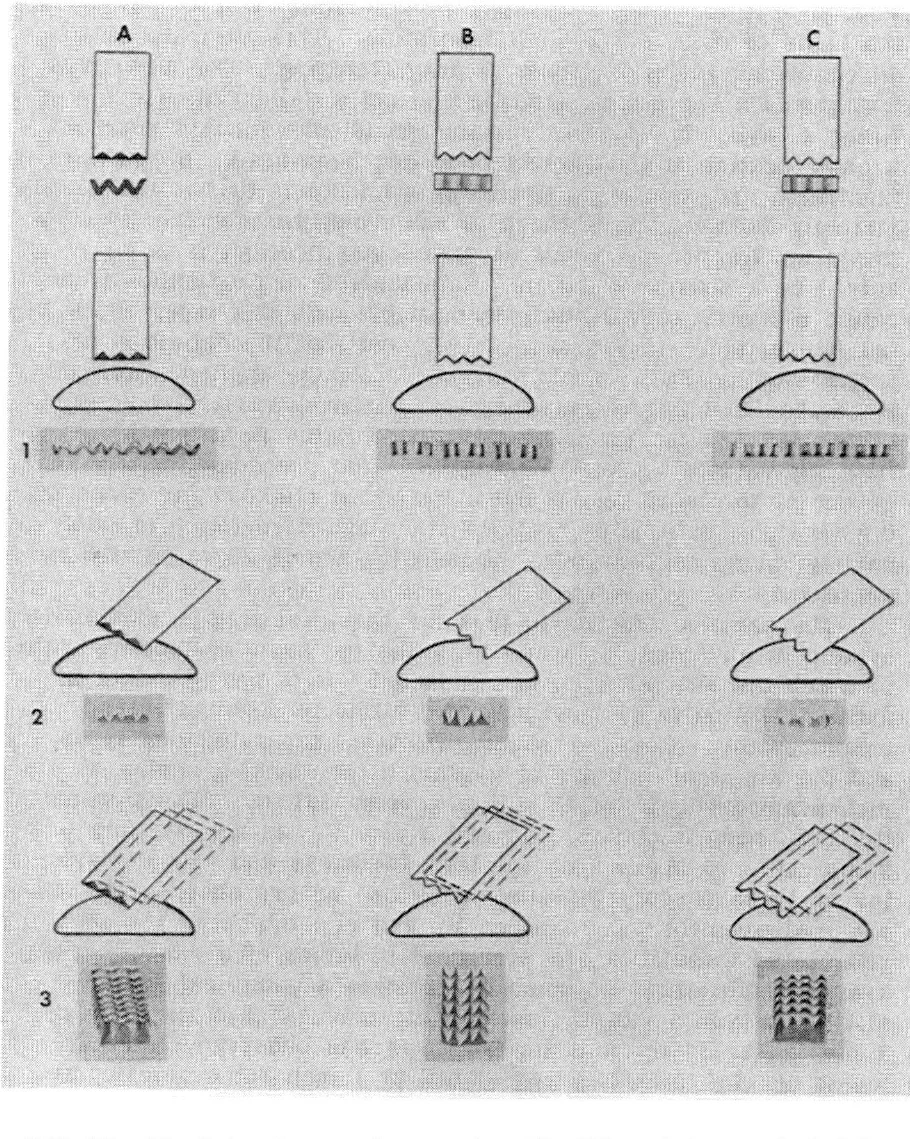

FIG. 10. Plasticine impressions made with different types of dentate tools, impressed at various angles: (A) pseudo-scallop shell tool, (B) pointed-notched tool, (C) blunt-notched tool, (1) vertical impressions, (2) oblique impressions, and (3) drag stamped impression.

a variety of pseudo-scallop shell will be proposed. Laurel Pseudo-scallop Shell, Naomikong Point variety, will be defined on the basis of obliquely applied decoration. This attribute is seen as equivalent to the attribute of drag stamping. The latter was considered a secondary attribute and not a valid criterion for defining a type. In order to remain consistent with this viewpoint, a classification at the variety level has been used. It has been mentioned that a prerequisite of an attribute is that it can be objectively defined. Since there is some dispute over the tool type producing the proposed new ceramic classification, it is conceived on a shaky foundation. Unfortunately, no established ceramic category seems totally compatible with this type. If, in the future, there is a general agreement that the definition of pseudo-scallop shell should embrace obliquely applied, alternately notched tool decoration, then this proposed variety could be eliminated. In the meantime, while its status is still being verified, the variety name will be used. This procedure appears to be one of the more successful abbreviated methods for conveying information. In a later section a thorough description of this variety, along with attribute frequencies and photographs will be presented.

The ceramic discussion thus far has attempted to establish a system of communication and to define the basic framework within which the analysis will be conducted. It is now possible to direct attention to the mechanics of attribute description and measurement. After the sherds had been separated into types and the minimum number of vessels determined, a series of measurements were made with a vernier caliper. These were: lip, rim, body thickness, and grit size. It was not possible in some cases to obtain data for body thickness and vessel diameter on those vessels represented by one or two sherds. At least one measurement was made on lip and rim thickness for each vessel and these data are presented in terms of a range and an average thickness. In general there was a good deal of consistency within a vessel, however in some cases a variation of 1 millimeter in lip and rim thickness was observed. Measurements on rim thickness were taken at 1 inch below the lip, although on small sherds it was sometimes necessary to decrease this distance. The overall scheme of decoration for Laurel ceramics seems to be one of decorating only the upper one-third of the vessel and leaving the remainder plain. Not one example of a vessel which could be positively identified as Laurel had cord-markings. Although a good deal of effort was directed towards vessel reconstruction, only a few vessels were reconstructed to a degree of completeness where the plain portion was present. This definitely limited the information on the thickness of this portion of the vessel. Similarly, only on a few of the more complete vessels could a rim diameter be estimated.

The total number of measurements made on grit size varied according to the number of vessels representing each type. A minimum of two readings was taken for each vessel and in most cases three. These included the largest and smallest observable grit as well as an intermediate size. A range in grit size is presented for each ceramic type and an average is given. In most cases a crushed granitic rock seems to have served as the temper. Other types of grit were relatively scarce and when present, always occurred with crushed granitic grit which constituted the predominant tempering material. No attempt was made to accurately determine what proportion of the volume of a sherd was grit.

While the different ceramic types could represent temporal, spatial, or cultural changes, it is also possible that they indicate functional differences. Vessel size is one criterion from which functional differences could be inferred. Since there were no complete vessels, and only a few were partially complete, this criterion could not be applied. Another possible functional indicator is the presence of a charred incrustation on the interior portion of the vessel. The term charred "food" will be used to describe this substance, although it has not been positively identified as food remains. Its location suggests that the contents of the vessel were subjected to lengthy simmering, thereby allowing a precipitate to form around the lip of the vessel. While no count was taken on the presence of charred "food" on plain body sherds, the impression is that such an occurrence was extremely rare. Each vessel was examined for charred "food," and the number displaying this characteristic is presented for each ceramic type.

It has been mentioned that there were no complete vessels in the Naomikong Point assemblage and thus it was difficult to determine vessel shape. This information, however, could be inferred from a number of partially reconstructed vessels. In general, vessel shape appears to be conical, and this is supported by 11 conical vessel bottoms in the collection. No other type of vessel bottom was recognized. A rough estimate of vessel volume was obtained by assuming the vessel shape could be approximated by a cone. For a few of the partially reconstructed vessels, the height could be extrapolated from the slope of the sides.

In general the rim diameter was found to be about three-fourths of the vessel height. As a crude approximation, Laurel vessels probably had a capacity of 2 to 6 liters.

Among the other nonmetrical attributes examined were rim profile and the arrangement of decorative motif. The former were separated into three groups: insloping, straight, and outsloping. Within each ceramic type the decoration was broken into four units. These were: interior decoration, lip decoration, rim decoration, and body decoration. The term body, in this case, does not refer to the undecorated portion of the vessel but refers to that decorated part below the rim. For a particular ceramic type, by definition, the decoration was applied with a similar class of tool. There were, however, several different patterns which the decoration could follow. The motif could be applied in horizontal, vertical, or oblique lines, or in combinations of these styles. In some cases the rim was decorated differently from the rest of the vessel. Another alternative was to decorate only the rim and leave the rest of the vessel plain. This gives a total of four attributes for body sherd decoration (including one negative attribute): (1) horizontal lines, (2) vertical lines, (3) oblique lines, and (4) plain body. The first three attributes can be applied to rim decoration, giving a total of twelve possible pairs of attribute combinations.

In addition to the different design patterns that could be produced by combining these various styles, two additional attributes cross-cut all ceramic types. These are bossing and punctates. Sometimes these terms are prefixed by the words internal and external, thereby establishing four distinct attributes. Since there is some discrepancy in the use of these terms by archaeologists I will define them as follows. Internal bossing refers to an impression made with a circular tool on the inside of the vessel. A resulting bump or "node" is produced on the exterior of the vessel by this operation. Some archaeologists distinguish this technique from internal punctations in that the latter do not puncture the clay sufficiently to raise a node. A complementary set of terms is used to refer to this type of decoration applied to the exterior of the vessel. In this case exterior bossing gives a node on the inside of the vessel while external punctates produce no nodes. In the Naomikong assemblage all internal punctates produced external nodes and these were called bosses. Exterior punctations, whether they raised a node or not, were called punctates.

The only attribute which has not been examined is drag stamping. The position taken on this attribute has already been discussed in detail and will not be elaborated upon further.

A total of five ceramic types and one variety will be presented for the Middle Woodland assemblage. An attempt has been made to anticipate the kinds of data that may prove useful to future investigators. Associated with the descriptions of three types, representing approximately 90 percent of the ceramic sample, is a matrix showing the frequencies of the more important attribute combinations. Figure 11 shows the rim profiles referred to in the type descriptions.

These descriptions are supplemented with photographs of representative sherds. In some cases, however, the photographs are biased because they depict only part of the total attribute range. This condition was dictated by the degree of preservation of the sherds. Unfortunately, many design elements were too faint to be distinguished in a photograph. Bossed sherds seemed particularly vulnerable to weathering, and their relative absence in the plates reflects this factor. The Late Woodland ceramic assemblage has already been adequately described in the literature (McPherron, 1967:86-123), therefore a formal description of the types will not be presented.

Type Descriptions

Type: Laurel Pseudo-scallop Shell

Illustrations: Plates III and IV.

Sample Size: 160 rim sherds and 544 body sherds representing a minimum of 93 vessels.

Temper: Crushed granitic rock. Particle size varies from 0.8 mm. to 8.0 mm. with an average of 2.5 mm.

Method of Manufacture: Uncertain. One vessel clearly indicates construction by coiling (Plate III).

Surface Finish: Vessels are smoothed on the interior and exterior except for one case of interior channeling.

Decoration: Appears to be the result of a tool alternately notched on one side and then the other. Several partially complete vessels indicate that usually only the upper one-third of the vessel is decorated. Most frequently the designs are in parallel horizontal or oblique rows with parallel vertical rows occurring less frequently. Sometimes the rim is treated as a distinct unit and the decoration is applied at a different angle than the main pattern. The average width of a design element is 1.7 mm. while the average distance between parallel rows is 2.0 mm. When the rim is treated as a distinct zone of decoration the width of this zone varies from 5 to 10 mm. with 7 mm. representing the average. About one-third of all vessels are decorated with a single row of circular punctates of bosses, but never both, encircling the rim. The former are more frequent, occurring twice as often. Both are placed an average of 17 mm. below the lip, the average punctate diameter

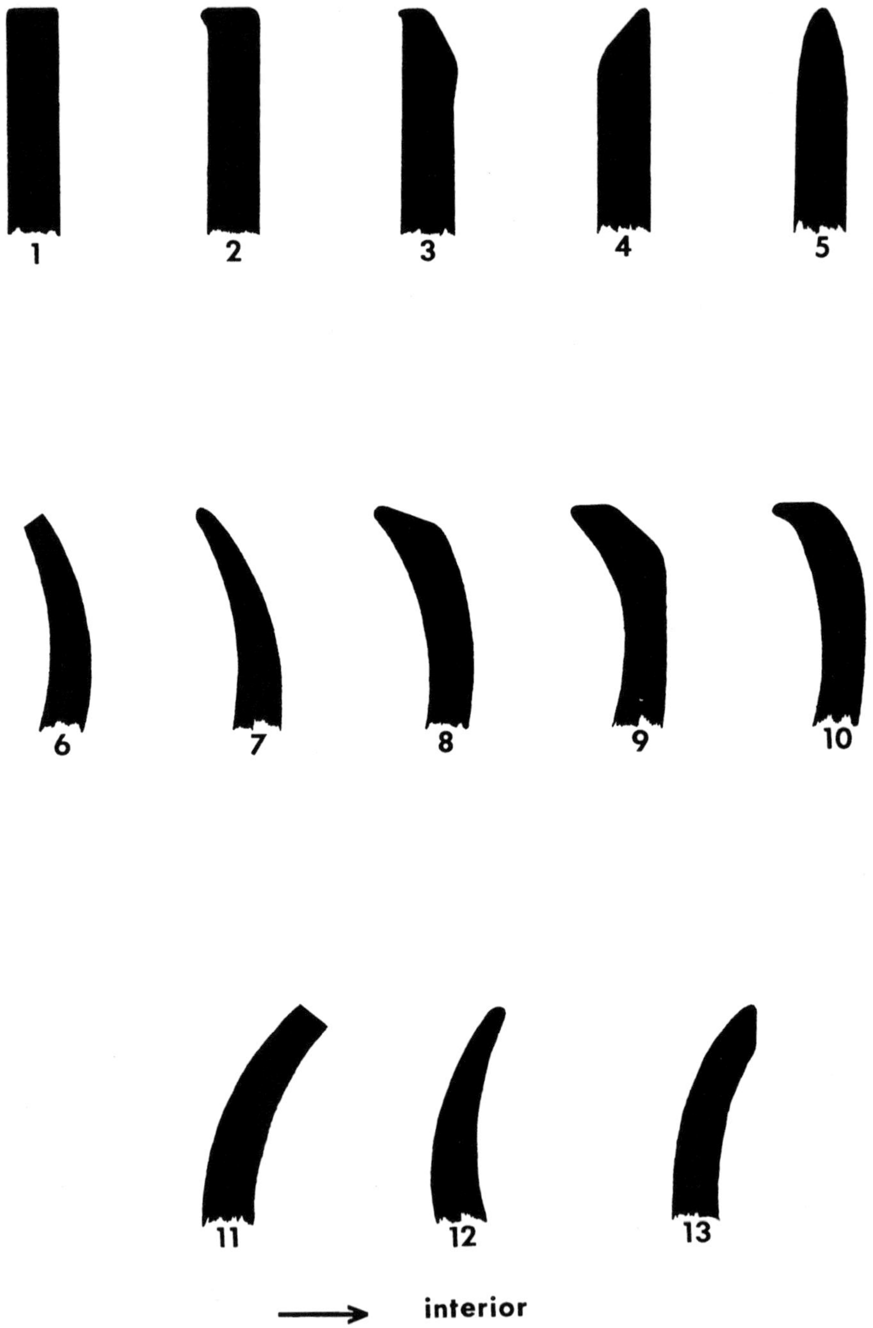

FIG. 11. Rim profiles.

being 3.2 mm. while the hole producing the boss is slightly larger with an average diameter of 3.7 mm. Lip treatment and interior decoration are other secondary decorative elements, the latter being infrequent and usually extending into the vessel an average of 10 mm.

Form: The most common lip shapes are flattened, rounded, or beveled, the first occurring with a frequency of 44 percent with the others at 27 percent and 28 percent respectively. Lip thickness varies from 2 mm. to 7 mm. with an average of 4 mm. Rim profiles can generally be classified as insloping, straight, and outsloping; the second being the most common. In Figure 11, profile 12 is the most frequent insloping profile at 67 percent. Profile 1 represents 41 percent of the straight rims with profiles 4 and 5 each having a frequency of about 20 percent. Finally, profile 6 is the most frequently occurring outsloping rim representing over half of this category. Rim thickness one inch below the lip, ranges from 4 mm. to 10 mm. with an average of 6.6 mm. Little data was present on the neck and shoulder, but neither appears to be accentuated. On those partially complete vessels the body thickness ranges from 5 mm. to 11 mm. with an average of 7 mm. Eight vessels are sufficiently complete to estimate rim diameter. This value varies from 15 cm. to 27 cm., with 20 cm. representing the average. Using these vessels, vessel shape is extrapolated as being conical.

Geographical Range: Southeastern Ontario, westward along the north shore of Lake Superior, northern Minnesota and extending into southeastern Manitoba. The southern limits include the Door Peninsula of Wisconsin and parts of the north shore of Lake Michigan.

Chronological Position: Middle Woodland.

Related Types: St. Lawrence Pseudo-scallop Shell of eastern Ontario and New York, and North Bay Scallop from the Door Peninsula of Wisconsin.

Remarks: Although the frequency of bossing is much lower than in the Minnesota sites, the same type of name has been retained since for this analysis, bossing is considered to be a secondary attribute. Caution must be taken in assuming that pseudo-scallop shell is the only decorative motif. Plate VII indicates that a row of small dentate elements can appear below the pseudo-scallop shell design. Other examples in the same plate show incised lines boardering the main decoration. This indicates that from body sherd examination alone two distinct types could erroneously be established. The interior of 15 vessels were coated with charred "food" remains. Refer to Table 4 for individual attribute frequencies as well as the frequency of co-occurrence of certain attribute pairs.

Type: Laurel Pseudo-scallop Shell—Naomikong Point Variety

Illustrations: Plates V and VI.

Sample Size: 97 rim sherds and 1,005 body sherds representing a minimum of 62 vessels.

Temper: Same as Laurel Pseudo-scallop Shell. The particle size ranged from 1.0 mm. to 9.0 mm. with an average of 2.6 mm.

TABLE 4

FREQUENCY OF ATTRIBUTE PAIRS FOR LAUREL PSEUDO-SCALLOP SHELL

	Rim A	Rim B	Rim C	Surface Treatment 1	2	3	4	Int. Dec.	Rim Treatment 1	2	3	4	Lip	Punc-tation	Boss-ing	Drag Stamping
	9	56	28	45	10	36	2	8	42	1	18	32	26	23	10	5
Rim A				7	1	1	0	0	2	0	4	3	0	1	0	0
Rim B				24	8	24	0	6	28	0	11	17	18	18	9	4
Rim C				14	1	11	2	2	12	1	3	12	8	4	1	1
Surface Treatment 1								3	3	0	17	25	9	4	9	0
Surface Treatment 2								0	8	0	1	1	4	2	1	0
Surface Treatment 3								5	29	1	0	6	13	17	0	5
Surface Treatment 4								0	2	0	0	0	0	0	0	0
Interior Decoration									4	0	1	3	1	3	1	0
Rim Treatment 1													14	15	1	3
Rim Treatment 2													1	0	0	0
Rim Treatment 3													4	2	5	0
Rim Treatment 4													7	6	4	2
Lip														8	4	1
Punctation															0	3
Bossing																0

Note: Rim: A = Insloping rim; B = Straight rim; C = Outsloping rim. Surface treatment: 1 = Horizontal body decoration; 2 = Vertical body decoration; 3 = Oblique body decoration; 4 = Plain body. Rim Treatment: 1 = Rim and body decorated alike; 2 = Horizontal rim decoration; 3 = Vertical rim decoration; 4 = Oblique rim decoration.

Method of Manufacture: Uncertain but some suggestion of coiling.

Surface Finish: Same as Laurel Pseudo-scallop Shell but no interior channeling.

Decoration: A tool similar to that used for Laurel Pseudo-scallop Shell appears to be used, although the notching does not seem to be restricted to alternate notching. The tool is always inserted into the clay at an acute angle. The decoration is applied in small units measuring approximately 5 mm. by 1 mm. Drag stamping is much more common than in Laurel Pseudo-scallop Shell, perhaps a factor of a smaller tool. In almost all cases the design consists of parallel horizontal rows of oblique elements. There is usually little separation between rows. Rim and lip decoration occur infrequently. The former can be treated as a distinct zone of decoration with the design applied at a different angle to the main pattern. In these instances the zone extends an average of 7 mm. below the lip, the same as for Laurel Pseudo-scallop Shell.

Bossing is almost entirely absent with only one example, however, nearly 25 percent of all vessels are decorated with a single row of circular punctates. Their size and placement on the vessel corresponds with the figures cited for Laurel Pseudo-scallop Shell. Interior decoration, executed with a notched tool, occurs at about the same frequency as punctation and extends into the vessel an average of 4 mm.

Form: Flattened lips predominate with a frequency of 57 percent followed by rounded lips at 24 percent. Lip thickness varies from 3 mm. to 6 mm. with those described for Laurel Pseudo-scallop Shell. Referring to Figure 11, 58 percent of the straight rims are profile 1 with 4 and 5 both representing about 17 percent. Profile 6 is the most frequent outsloping profile with a frequency of 50 percent, the same as found for Laurel Pseudo-scallop Shell. Finally, only 2 examples of an insloping profile are present, one of profile 11 and the other of profile 12. Rim thickness varies from 5 mm. to 9 mm. with an average of 7 mm. Data pertaining to vessel neck, shoulder, and body are the same as for Laurel Pseudo-scallop Shell. An estimated vessel diameter of 19 cm. is obtained from one vessel. Vessel shape cannot be determined from the sample, however it is probably the same as Laurel Pseudo-scallop Shell.

Geographical Range: Uncertain. Similar ceramics occur in northern Ontario and the Door Peninsula of Wisconsin, as well as northern Minnesota.

Chronological Position: Same as Laurel Pseudo-scallop Shell.

Related Types: Complex Stab and Drag (Mason, 1967). Laurel Push-pull (Stoltman, 1962), and Nutimik Oblique (MacNeish, 1958).

Remarks: Although several related types are defined by the attribute of drag stamping this is not a prerequisite of this type. Plate VII indicates that incised lines sometimes occur below the main decorative pattern. A similar secondary treatment was observed on Laurel Pseudo-scallop Shell and the same statements presented in that discussion apply here. Twenty vessels contained charred "food" remains. Table 5 indicates attribute frequencies and the frequency of certain attribute combinations.

Type: Laurel Linear Stamp

Illustrations: Plate VIII.

Sample Size: 148 rim sherds and 1,360 body sherds representing a minimum of 102 vessels.

Temper: Same as Laurel Pseudo-scallop Shell. Particle size varied from 0.7 mm. to 7.0 mm. with an average of 2.3 mm.

Method of Manufacture: Uncertain, but some suggestions of coiling.

Surface Finish: Smoothed interior and exterior.

Decoration: An unnotched tool is used to produce a linear or slightly curved element. Simple stamping may be a better descriptive term for this method than linear stamping. Elements tend to be of a consistent size for any one vessel, but may vary in length from 4 mm. to 9 mm.

TABLE 5

FREQUENCY OF ATTRIBUTE PAIRS FOR LAUREL PSEUDO-SCALLOP SHELL NAOMIKONG POINT VARIETY

	Rim A	Rim B	Rim C	Surface Treatment 1	Surface Treatment 2	Surface Treatment 3	Surface Treatment 4	Int. Dec.	Rim Treatment 1	Rim Treatment 2	Rim Treatment 3	Rim Treatment 4	Lip	Punc-tation	Boss-ing	Drag Stamping
	2	21	19	3	12	44	3	21	47	0	0	7	21	20	1	23
Rim A				0	1	0	1	0	1	0	0	1	0	1	0	1
Rim B				3	8	23	1	17	27	0	4	4	13	12	1	17
Rim C				0	3	21	1	4	19	0	5	2	8	7	0	5
Surface Treatment 1								3	3	0	0	0	2	3	0	2
Surface Treatment 2								2	8	0	2	2	0	3	0	2
Surface Treatment 3								16	36	0	6	3	18	14	1	19
Surface Treatment 4								0	0	0	1	2	1	0	0	0
Interior Decoration									18	0	1	2	13	12	0	11
Rim Treatment 1													17	5	1	17
Rim Treatment 2													0	0	0	0
Rim Treatment 3													3	3	0	3
Rim Treatment 4													1	2	0	3
Lip														8	0	10
Punctation															0	9
Bossing																0

Note: See note, Table 4.

A fairly constant width of about 1 mm. is maintained throughout. Since no partially complete vessels are present it is not possible to determine what proportion of the vessel is decorated. Horizontal rows of oblique elements are the predominant decorative pattern with horizontal rows of vertical elements forming a minority design. The average distance between rows is 2 mm. Rims are sometimes treated as distinct zones of decoration but less frequently than pseudo-scallop shell types. In these cases the decorated area extends 5 mm. to 8 mm. below the lip. Only one example of bossing is present, whereas a single row of circular punctates occurs on approximately 15 percent of the vessels. Punctate diameter varies from 2.0 to 2.5 mm. and placement is usually 14 mm. below the lip. Interior decoration and lip treatment occur at about the same frequency and are found on 10 percent of the vessels. The former usually extend into the vessel from 4 mm. to 8 mm.

Form: The most common lip shape is flattened, representing 70 percent of all vessels. Beveled lips are absent. Lip thickness varies from 3 mm. to 8 mm. with an average of 4.6 mm. Rim profiles correspond to those described for Laurel Pseudo-scallop Shell, with straight and outsloping being the most common forms. Profile 1 in Figure 11 represents 69 percent of the straight rims while 2 and 5 are secondary profiles each occurring with a frequency of 13 percent. Eighty percent of all outsloping rims are profile 6 while insloping rim profiles are equally divided between 11 and 12. Rim thicknesses ranges between 5 mm. and 12 mm. with an average of 6.5 mm. Data pertaining to neck, shoulder, and body are limited to two vessels, both of which have slightly constricted necks, gently rounded shoulders, and a body thickness of 8 mm. Below the main decorated portion of both vessels are parallel vertically incised lines. No determination of vessel shape is possible. The average rim diameter, based on four vessels, is 23 cm.

Geographical Range: Similar ceramics have been described by Wright (1967) from the north shore of Lake Superior. The western limits include northern Minnesota, while the northern parts of Lake Michigan define the southern limits.

Chronological Position: Middle Woodland.

Related Types: North Bay Linear Stamped from the Porte des Mortes site on the Door Peninsula of Wisconsin appears to have a generic relationship with this type, as well as Lockport Linear as defined by MacNeish (1958:145). The type Simple Stab and drag (Mason, 1967) may be applied to the drag stamp sherds of Laurel Linear Stamped as used in this analysis. A group of ten sherds, all apparently from the same vessel, showed a striking similarity to a partially complete vessel from Summer Island in northern Lake Michigan. Brose (personal communication) classifies this vessel as Upper Peninsula Dragged Stamp. Plate IX shows the Summer Island vessel contrasted with a sherd from Naomikong Point.

Remarks: Table 6 presents attribute frequencies as well as the frequencies of certain attribute pairs. Twenty-three vessels contain charred "food" remains.

Type: Laurel Plain

Illustrations: Plate X.

Sample Size: 51 rim sherds and an undetermined number of body sherds representing a minimum of 25 vessels.

Temper: Same as Laurel Pseudo-scallop Shell. Particle size varied from 1.0 mm. to 8.0 mm. with an average of 2.8 mm.

Method of Manufacture: Uncertain, but several vessels indicate fractures along coil lines.

Surface Finish: Smoothed interior and exterior.

Decoration: This type lacks external decoration although bossing may be present. Lip decoration as well as internal designs are absent in the Naomikong Point assemblage.

Form: Straight rims with flattened or rounded lips predominate, although two outsloping rims and one insloping rim are present. The lip thickness varies from 2 mm. to 7 mm. with an average of 4 mm., while rim thickness ranges from 8 mm. to 12 mm. with an average of 7 mm. The diameter of the interior punctates producing the bosses is 4 mm. No data on neck, shoulder, or body are present. On the basis of three vessels, an average rim diameter of 10 cm. is obtained.

TABLE 6

FREQUENCY OF ATTRIBUTE PAIRS FOR LAUREL LINEAR STAMP

	Rim			Surface Treatment				Int. Dec.	Rim Treatment				Lip	Punc-tation	Boss-ing	Drag Stamping
	A	B	C	1	2	3	4		1	2	3	4				
	8	45	36	0	7	70	12	13	62	1	14	12	17	17	1	35
Rim A				0	1	4	3	1	3	1	1	3	0	1	1	2
Rim B				0	4	36	5	6	34	0	6	5	9	13	0	20
Rim C				0	2	30	4	6	25	0	7	4	8	3	0	13
Surface Treatment 1								0	0	0	0	0	0	0	0	0
Surface Treatment 2								0	5	0	0	2	2	2	1	0
Surface Treatment 3								12	56	1	12	1	14	13	0	33
Surface Treatment 4								1	1	0	2	9	1	2	0	2
Interior Decoration									8	0	4	1	1	4	0	5
Rim Treatment 1													15	13	1	27
Rim Treatment 2													0	0	0	0
Rim Treatment 3													1	2	0	6
Rim Treatment 4													1	2	0	2
Lip														3	0	3
Punctation															0	9
Bossing																0

Note: See note Table 4.

Geographical Range: Present on all Laurel sites.

Chronological Position: Middle Woodland.

Related Types: Lockport Plain (MacNeish, 1958:150). Laurel Bossed and Laurel Nondecorated (Stoltman, 1962) have been combined in this analysis into Laurel Plain.

Remarks: A total of three vessels contain charred "food" remains.

Type: Laurel Dentate

Illustrations: Plate XI (*a–d*).

Sample Size: 16 body sherds representing an estimated 3 to 5 vessels.

Temper: Same as Laurel Pseudo-scallop Shell. Particle size varies from 0.1 mm. to 0.5 mm. with an average of 2.1 mm.

Method of Manufacture: Coiling is suggested by 6 sherds.

Surface Finish: Smoothed interior and exterior.

Decoration: The design is produced by inserting a notched tool into the clay producing several elements in a single operation. Each element is rectangular with rounded corners, and measures approximately

1.5 mm. by 1.0 mm. Since the Naomikong Point sample is composed of body sherds, a pattern cannot be precisely defined, but decoration appears to run in horizontal lines.

Form: Uncertain. The body sherds have an average thickness of 6 mm.

Geographical Range: Found on all Laurel sites as well as the ceramic assemblages from neighboring cultures to the east and south.

Related Types: North Bay Dentate may be related to this type. As indicated above, the wide geographical range of dentate stamping gives many possible related types.

Type: Laurel Incised

Illustrations: Plate XI (*e*).

Sample Size: One rim sherd representing one vessel (see remarks).

Temper: Same as Laurel Pseudo-scallop Shell. Particle size varies from 0.9 mm to 4.0 mm. with an average of 2.0 mm.

Method of Manufacture: Uncertain.

Surface Finish: Smoothed interior and exterior.

Decoration and Form: A single row of prominent bosses encircle the rim. The lip is flattened and the rim outsloping as shown in Figure 11, profile 6. The lip measures 4 mm., the rim thickness 6 mm. and the diameter of the holes producing the bossing is 4 mm.

Remarks: This sherd conforms precisely with the type as defined by Stoltman (1962). As pointed out earlier, and illustrated in Plate VII, incising can also occur as a secondary motif with Pseudo-scallop Shell. This means that caution should be exercised in attempting to identify this type by body sherds alone. The body sherds shown in Plate XI (*f-m*) do not necessarily represent Laurel Incised sherds and most likely are a secondary motif.

Late Woodland Pottery

The preceding type descriptions relate to that portion of the assemblage that can be classified as Middle Woodland. A group of Late Woodland sherds were also recovered and the majority are characterized by cord decoration and cord-wrapped paddle impressions. This category is composed of 1,089 sherds which can be broken down into 928 cord-marked body sherds, 78 cord-decorated body sherds, and 83 cord-decorated rim sherds. These counts are for sherds with a length greater than one inch and this represents approximately 6 percent of the total ceramic sample. The Late Woodland ceramic assemblage appears to have strong affinities with pottery from the Juntunen site on Bois Blanc Island in the Straits of Mackinac. The ceramic typology established by McPherron (1967) for Juntunen embraces the Naomikong

Point material, and this was confirmed by McPherron who personally examined the collection. The greater part of this sample can be grouped within the ceramic classification of Mackinac Ware. The latter is composed of five types, three of which (Mackinac Undecorated, Mackinac Punctate, and Mackinac Cord-impressed) are present at Naomikong Point. These are represented by a minimum of 51 vessels derived from 83 rim sherds. Crushed granitic rock serves as the tempering material and ranges in size from 1 to 10 mm. Vessels display thickened lips of 6 to 11 mm. thinning to 5 to 8 mm. one inch below the lip. Data pertaining to the remainder of the vessel could not be derived from the sample. Interior decoration, consisting of vertical cord impressions, is present on 70 percent of the vessels. An average vessel diameter of 20 cm. is based on measurements from 3 vessels. Charred "food" remains occur on 27 vessels. Plates XII and XIV*a* illustrate Mackinac ware rim sherds from Naomikong Point.

The remainder of the Late Woodland ceramics consists of 24 sherds. Included in this are 17 fabric-impressed body sherds (Plate XI *n*-*p*). Not only is Mackinac ware characterized by a surface finish of cord-wrapped-paddle impressions, but occasionally fabric impressions are found. It is therefore likely that these fabric-impressed sherds should be included within the Mackinac ware category. Finally, 4 rim sherds, representing 4 vessels are assignable to Bois Blanc ware (Plate XIII *a*, *b*), and 2 rim sherds, representing 2 vessels can be classified as Juntunen ware (Plate XIII *c*, *d*) (McPherron, 1967:104-16). These sherds are illustrated in Plate XVI. One Huron Incised vessel (Plate XIV*b*), consisting of 4 rim sherds completes the Late Woodland ceramic assemblage.

Aboriginal Clay Pipes

Two sections of an aboriginal clay pipe were recovered from the midden in unit 485 E 365; a pipe bowl and a stem. While these do not fit together they appear to represent the same pipe with an intermediate section missing. The clay is reddish-orange in color and displays a crushed granitic temper with an average size of 4 mm. The bowl shape is that of a truncated cone with a length of 4.9 cm., a maximum diameter of 3.1 cm. at the top, tapering to a diameter of 1.8 cm. at the base. The shape of the interior of the bowl follows that of the exterior and has a depth of 2.6 cm. The upper diameter is 1.7 cm. while at the bottom of the bowl the diameter is 0.7 cm. The interior of the bowl extends vertically through the base, and the stem probably joined at this point although this part of the pipe is missing. It is not possible to reconstruct the angle the stem made with the bowl or the total length of the stem. That portion recovered is 5.4 cm. in length. The cross section of the stem is circular, the end near the bowl having a diameter of 1.5; the stem hole is circular with a mean diameter of 2.5 mm. Along one side of the stem are two horizontal rows of obliquely-incised, or simple tool-impressed decoration. Plate XV *a, b* illustrates both the bowl and the stem.

STONE INDUSTRY

Introduction

An analysis of the stone industry can be broken into two basic sections. These deal with, (1) finished stone artifacts, and (2) the chippage debris derived from artifact production. The former can be divided into two parts: chipped-stone artifacts manufactured from flints, and rough stone artifacts fashioned by modifying natural forms of igneous and sedimentary rock. The availability of these materials to aboriginal populations at Naomikong Point deserves some comments. Rough stone artifacts can be dispensed with most easily. The shore of Lake Superior furnishes a ready supply of material for artifact manufacture making the importation of stone for hammerstone, celt, pestle, and net sinker production unnecessary. To some extent the same remarks pertain to flint material, however, a wide range of flint types is represented in the stone assemblage. No single type seems to predominate; cherts range in color from white, through shades of gray to black, as well as browns, tans, and pinks. White, yellow, and brownish quartzites are also present. In general this spectrum of colored cherts and quartzites can be expected since the local sources are glacially derived. During glacial periods flint from distant localities was sometimes brought together and deposited in a single region, which seems to best explain the presence of the variety of flint types at Naomikong Point. While this is only a working hypothesis, one type of material is definitely not locally derived, nor is its presence the result of glacial activity. This material is obsidian. Six small, unworked obsidian flakes were recovered from the midden, and two of these were subjected to neutron activation analysis at the University of Michigan Neutron Activation Laboratory. The process involves bombarding a known weight of obsidian with thermal neutrons and observing the decay products and their counts. By comparing this data with those obtained from samples whose sources are known, it is possible to determine the origin of the test specimen. Analyses run on the two Naomikong Point obsidian flakes indicate that they are derived from the Obsidian Cliff 150 Group in Yellowstone Park. These data conform with the results obtained on other obsidian samples from the Middle West for Middle Woodland sites (Griffin *et al.*, n.d.).

In summary, aside from a few specimens of obsidian, all material for the production of chipped-stone artifacts appears to be locally derived. A small amount of Eastport chert and a projectile point made from a dull pink chert (Plate XVII*a*) may be possible exceptions. Every flint chip and flint artifact was individually examined, and this degree of involvement with the lithic assemblage did not reveal any persistent flint type in the collection. Another clue pointing towards local resources is obtained from the chippage analysis which appears below.

Chippage Analysis

The processing of raw material for artifact production yields an aggregation of chippage debris which displays distinctive characteristics for the various stages of manufacture. Three basic steps in the making of flake tools can be delineated, although it should be understood that this is a generalization and does not apply in all cases. The initial process involves the removal of cortex, or modification of the raw material. Next, smaller flakes are derived, and from these the artifact is fashioned. Since these steps can be carried out in different locations, knowing the chipping types associated with each operation allows task-specific areas to be recognized. Furthermore, in making different types of artifacts, different kinds of chippage may be derived.

The utility of chippage analyses in deriving temporal, spatial, and cultural information has been pointed out by various archaeologists, and several schemes for defining chippage types have been presented. Witthoff (1957) discusses the problem in detail, and other thorough treatments are found in Binford and Quimby (1963), Fitting, DeVisscher, and Wahla (1966) and McPherron (1967). The most serious problem confronting the archaeologist in carrying out this type of analysis is to define the criteria for establishing the various categories of chippage. The foremost consideration is that the criteria can be objectively defined and are mutually exclusive. Both requirements are difficult to achieve, and as will be shown later, a degree of subjectivity enters the analysis.

The number of chippage categories established is to some extent dictated by the material. Fitting (*in* Fitting, DeVisscher, and Wahla, 1966) has devised a breakdown for chippage and cores which are derived from small chert nodules, a material commonly found in Upper Great Lakes chipping stations. This classification is considered the most desirable one for handling the Naomikong Point chippage. According to this system the chippage is divided into four main categories: (1) decortication flakes, (2) block flakes, (3) flakes with striking platforms, and (4) flat flakes. Two types of cores are delineated: (1) small cores and (2) block cores. The first chippage category represents those flakes removed from the exterior of the nodule. In this process the cortex is flaked away revealing the flint, and it is the presence of cortex that defines this type of chippage (Plate XVI*a*). Block flakes may, or may not, be the result of intentional knapping. They are irregular in shape, and are formed by either rough trimming or frost or heat fractures along natural flaws in the material (Plate XVI*b*). Small sections of cortex may be present on block flakes as well as flakes in categories (3) and (4). This means that the defining criteria for decortication flakes overlap into the other categories. This problem is resolved by requiring decortication flakes to have a relatively larger cortex surface than the other categories. It is understandable that all cortex will not be removed in the initial operation, and to rigidly adhere to the requirement that the presence of cortex equals decortication flake is impractical. In only 5 or 10 percent of the cases will there be a problem in classifying a flake as decortication or block, and these cases must be resolved by subjective judgment.

The third chippage category, flat flakes (Plate XVI*d*), is to some extent self explanatory. These flakes are small and flat, and are recognized by the absence of a striking platform. Many of them are probably remnants of larger flakes with platforms which fractured off during the knapping process. The last category of chippage includes flakes with striking platforms, and these can be subdivided into several smaller units. A major separation into two parts can be made on the basis of the tool used in deriving the flakes. Hard hammer flakes are those produced with a stone tool. Characteristics of this group include a prominent bulb of percussion, an impact scar at the striking platform, fracture scars along the cone of percussion, and no lip or overhang on the interior of the flake (Plate XVI*f*). Soft hammer flakes (Plate XVI*e*) are struck with a bone, horn, or wooden hammer, and a distinctive feature is a lip or overhang, on the interior surface of the flake projecting out from the striking platform. There is a relatively smaller bulb of percussion and fewer shatter marks along the cone of percurssion than in hard hammer flakes. A subclass of soft hammer flakes are those which seem to have been struck from a bifacially-worked object. These flakes are termed flakes of bifacial retouch (Plate XVI*g*). Their distinguishing feature is that the angle between the striking platform and the exterior of the flake is acute. The intersection of these two surfaces frequently shows evidence of grinding.

Cores are divided into two types for this analysis. The first of these is small bipolar cores. These are derived from small beach pebbles which are chipped by a hammer and anvil technique. A percussion blow directed at the top of the core is followed by a momentum transfer from the anvil to the bottom of the core. This can impart sufficient energy to produce shattering at the base. For the bipolar core, the basal shattering can then serve as a prepared striking platform for deriving flakes (Plate XVI*c*). Block cores represent the second core category. These cores are much larger than those in the first group, and they are characterized by relatively flat, straight sides from which flakes are removed.

Using the above outlined procedure a total of 20,284 pieces of unworked chippage and 676 cores from Naomikong Point were subjected to examination. A breakdown into chippage types is presented in Table 7. Several points in the analysis deserve further comment. First, the cortex surface of the decortication flakes showed a marked curvature, and the impression gained is that pebbles in the size range of tennis balls were the most

TABLE 7

FREQUENCIES OF FLAKE AND CORE TYPES

Types	Frequency	Percent
Decortication flakes	2,946	14.5
Block flakes	5,993	29.9
Hard hammer flakes	616	3.0
Soft hammer flakes	728	3.6
Flake of bifacial retouch	1,241	6.1
Flat flake	8,741	43.0
Total flakes	20,284	100.0
Bipolar cores	342	50.6
Block cores	199	29.4
Core fragments	135	19.0
Total cores	676	100.0

frequently utilized. The very presence of such a large number of decortication flakes, 2,946, as well as all the by-product flakes of flint knapping, indicates that the entire manufacturing process, from raw material to finished artifact, was carried out at the site. Moreover, the similarity of the decortication flakes with beach pebbles from the lake shore further substantiates the claim that locally derived materials were being exploited. The high percentage of bipolar cores, associated with the postulated small pebble utilization, is a verification of Fitting's hypothesis (*in* Fitting, DeVisscher, and Wahla, 1966) that the bipolar core technique is used for working small nodules. This points up some earlier remarks that the definition of chippage categories is dependent upon the technique of processing the material. Bipolar chipping serves as a good example.

It will be noted in Table 7 that no unipolar cores are represented. Aside from block cores, which are easy to identify, all other cores showed bipolar chipping. In the category of core fragments, which seems to represent exhausted cores, some unipolar examples are present. However, because of their fragmentary nature they were eliminated from the sample. Perhaps there is some divergence in what Fitting has called unipolar cores and the way they were considered in this analysis. Nevertheless, the most important inference to be derived from either the unipolar or bipolar core is that both techniques are used with small pebble chipping.

A number of bipolar cores had been modified and converted into tools by working one end to a chisel-like edge. The Old World term *piece esquillée* is sometimes applied to this type of tool, whose function was probably that of a bone-splitting implement. It was often difficult to determine if the cutting, or splitting edge was; intentionally formed, derived as a by-product of a flake, or part of a prepared striking platform. A total of 64 cores could be identified as tools with certainty, however, many others were possible candidates.

In analyzing the chippage, two characteristics unrelated to the actual chipping technique were recorded. One of these was the presence of pock marks or "pot-lids." The latter are small rounded spalls that are the result of frost activity or heat action. As pointed out at the 1964 Conference on Lithic Technology, Les Eyzies, France (unpublished notes) the heat treatment of flint induces certain properties which add to its workability. Since "pot-lids" may imply intentional heat treating, all chippage was examined for these marks. A total of 1,652 flakes displayed this feature. The other characteristic examined was quartzite chippage. This material occurred throughout the site although only 54 artifacts were recovered. A count was made on all quartzite chippage and the total was 1,843. Counts on both heat-treated flakes and quartzite chippage are recorded for each five-by-five unit. In the next chapter their distribution, as well as their correlation with other artifact categories will be discussed.

Projectile Points

Considering the total number of flint artifacts recovered from the 2,750 square feet excavated at Naomikong Point, projectile points are relatively scarce. The site yielded only 49, of which 33 were complete. Four main types of projectile points can be distinguished. One is a side-notched point with a flaring convex base that shows some resemblance to the Stott Corner-notched point (MacNeish, 1954:40). Fifteen projectile points of this type are represented in the collection, part of which are illustrated in (Plate XVII *c-o*).

Other projectile points include 11 corner-notched (Plate XVII *a, b*) and four stemmed (Plate XVII *p-r*). One large point made of a dull pinkish chert, shows basal grinding (Plate XVII*a*), and is very similar to the Snyder's point of Illinois Hopewell. There are also eight triangular points in the collection that are characteristic of the widely distributed Late Woodland triangular point which has a wide geographical distribution. Six of these points, or 75 percent occur in that part of the site with the greatest concentration of Late Woodland pottery. Measurements on all complete projectile points are given in Table 8.

Preforms

Twenty-one preforms, sometimes referred to as bifacial blades, unnotched bifaces, or blanks, are represented in this artifact category. This number includes nine broken specimens. All were found singly; there was no indication that any of them were part of a cache. The material coincides with that used in manufacturing projectile points. No one type of stone dominates the assemblage. As with projectile points, quartzite was not utilized. Most are nicely worked and thinned, and only a few examples are crude. There is no evidence of basal grinding and it does not appear that these artifacts were subjected to usage. All measurement data are presented in Table 9, and Plate XVIII illustrates a sample collection. Specimen *d* is made of Eastport chert.

TABLE 8

METRIC ATTRIBUTES OF PROJECTILE POINTS
(In Centimeters)

Catalogue Numbers	Length	Hafting Width	Maximum Width	Thickness	Weight (gm.)
Corner notched					
72618	3.4	1.7	2.9	1.2	10
72723	3.9	0.8	1.9	0.7	4
72747	8.0	2.0	5.8	1.1	5
72828	4.6	1.5	2.4	0.7	8
72933	2.7	1.1	1.5	0.4	2
76302	4.3	1.1	2.0	0.8	6
76321	3.0	1.1	1.8	0.8	4
76323	2.0	1.2	1.6	0.4	1
76415	2.6	0.6	1.5	0.6	2
76455	4.0	1.2	2.1	0.7	4
76531	5.2	1.3	2.5	1.1	15
Side notched					
72612	5.0	1.0	2.2	0.7	6
72699	4.4	1.0	2.2	0.6	5
72752	4.4	1.3	2.5	0.6	6
72786	8.2	2.2	3.0	0.9	20
72806	4.6	1.2	1.4	0.8	4
72937	3.3	1.1	1.7	0.5	4
76327	1.8	0.9	1.1	0.2	1
76455	2.7	1.1	1.7	0.7	2
76464	2.3	1.0	1.3	0.4	1
76530	4.8	1.3	2.0	0.6	6
Stemmed					
72618	5.5	1.6	3.3	1.2	18
76060	4.5	1.1	2.3	0.8	6
76071	4.7	1.2	2.3	0.7	5
76309	4.0	1.1	2.1	0.7	6
Triangular					
72677	2.3	...	1.3	0.5	1
72857	2.1	...	1.6	0.4	1
76116	2.6	...	1.7	0.3	2
76247	2.4	...	1.7	0.4	2
76322	6.4	...	2.8	0.8	12
76363	7.3	...	2.9	0.8	14
76415	1.8	...	1.4	0.4	1
76457	2.4	...	1.4	0.2	1

Scrapers

Next to pottery, scrapers are the most numerous artifacts. A total of 1,882 was recovered, or an average of about 18 per 5- by 5-foot unit. They were relatively evenly distributed over the

TABLE 9

METRIC ATTRIBUTES OF PREFORMS
(In Centimeters)

Catalogue Numbers	Length	Width	Thickness
72660	4.2	2.1	0.5
72933	5.0	2.3	0.7
72973	4.6	2.4	0.8
76247	5.0	2.9	0.8
76267	4.3	2.3	0.7
76289	4.6	2.9	0.6
76297	6.0	2.3	0.6
76313	5.0	2.9	0.7
76322	6.4	2.8	0.8
76345	5.1	2.3	0.6
76348	4.3	2.8	0.8
76363	7.3	2.8	0.7

site and were associated with all types of chippage. In both size and shape there is a great deal of variation. Several classes of scraping edges are discernible, ranging from linear to angular, both of which can be continuous or discontinuous. There are examples of retouch along two parallel edges as well as flaking around the entire perimeter of the flake. Usually retouch is produced on the opposite side of the flake from the bulb of percussion but there are some exceptions. Hard hammer, soft hammer, decortication, and flat flakes have all been converted into scrapers and occasionally a scraper is made on a flake of bifacial retouch. Chert is the predominant material utilized, with quartzite used in only fourteen cases. Crosscutting all these categories is size. Scraper length varies continuously from about one to four centimeters, with weights ranging from one gram to 20 grams.

The amount of diversity described above makes it extremely difficult to apply a typology to scrapers. A threefold division was made following a rather standard terminology. End scrapers were established as that class of scrapers in which the retouch is perpendicular to the axis of the flake. The latter is not necessarily the maximum length of the flake, although it may be, and is defined as the axis running from the striking platform through the bulb of percussion. For most cases the axis of the flake is the same as the axis of the tool, however, a slight amount of drifting is allowed. This deviates from some Old World Paleolithic typologies where such deviations may be significant in defining types. For the Naomikong Point scrapers, as long as part of the retouch was perpendicular to the axis of the flake, they were classified as end scrapers. Modifications of this defining criterion may be necessary in some cases and these will be discussed later. Most frequently end scrapers are fan-shaped, although ovate and circular forms are present. In some rare instances the worked surface is at the same end as the bulb of percussion. A total of 1,288 end scrapers were in the collection.

The second class of scrapers is side scrapers. Members of this group are retouched on one side of the flake only, and this side is parallel or oblique to the axis of the flake. Many of the same remarks concerning end scrapers apply to side scrapers. This latter category is less frequent in the collection, and only 151 examples are present. There appears to be somewhat more diversity in the shape of side scrapers because a variety of different kinds of flakes was used. As with end scrapers, chert is the most common material and quartzite is utilized only four times.

The third class of scrapers is actually for those examples that cannot be placed into the first two groups. In discussing end scrapers it was mentioned that the retouch should be approximately perpendicular to the axis of the flake, but this is not a sufficient condition. Some scrapers display retouch on more than one face of the flake; these will be referred to as multifaced scrapers. This retouch can be either continuous or discontinuous. The former can display chipping along one side continuing around the end of the flake, thus combining the defining attributes for side and end scrapers. In some cases the entire perimeter of the flake is retouched. Discontinuous multifaced scrapers display chipping on two, three, or four sides of the flake. Since retouch is not limited to either the end or the side of a flake, but displays a variety of patterns, it is difficult to define scraper types objectively. The various kinds of multifaced scrapers are not divided into subtypes, but all 182 examples are considered as a single group. In general, other than displaying multiple retouch, their characteristics, such as flake size and flake shape, show the same degree of variability as found among end and side scrapers.

It has been mentioned that scrapers are made on all types of chippage and one particular type of flake, the decortication flake, is utilized 478 times. Decortication flakes require the minimum amount of time to be produced since they are the first chippage by-product in flake production. The conversion of this type of flake to a scraper may indicate an immediate need for a tool; however, this is of course speculation.

A sample of end and side scrapers was subjected to microscopic examination to see if there were any usage patterns. The results indicate a series of small flake scars along the basal portion of the retouched edge which may be the consequence of usage. The rear portion of several end scrapers show minute flake fractures as if the artifact had been hafted. The extremely small size of some end scrapers implies that hafting may have been the only way they could be utilized.

Because of the size of the sample, measurements were not made on every scraper but were taken on a sample of 300 end scrapers and 100 side scrapers. Table 10 gives the ranges and averages of these measurements. Plate XIX illustrates a sample of end scrapers.

TABLE 10

RANGES AND AVERAGES OF ATTRIBUTES FROM A SAMPLING OF SCRAPERS

Scrapers	Range	Average
End scrapers		
(Sample - 300)		
Overall length (cm.)	3.7-1.1	2.1
Width (cm.)	3.3-1.2	2.0
Thickness (cm.)	1.0-0.2	0.4
Length of worked edge (cm.)	10.0-1.2	2.8
Arc of worked edge (degrees)	360-20	84.2
Weight (gm.)	8.5-0.3	2.2
Side scrapers		
(Sample - 100)		
Overall length (cm.)	2.5-0.8	1.5
Width (cm.)	3.4-1.6	2.2
Thickness of edge (cm.)	0.8-0.1	0.3
Length of edge (cm.)	5.0-1.2	2.2
Weight (gm.)	4.9-0.4	1.7

Drills

Drills are scarce at Naomikong Point and only five are represented in the collection. All but one are broken and this is a quartzite artifact which may be a graver (Plate XVIII*n*). Two drill tips were subjected to microscopic examination, and there was evidence of polish on the crests of the flake scars but not in the flake scar depressions. This pattern was observed on all parts of the tip suggesting a rotary motion and verifying that these artifacts may have indeed served as drills. Because of the fragmentary nature of the sample no measurements were taken. Plate XVIII *l-p* illustrates all drills recovered from the site.

Retouched Flakes

This category includes all those pieces of chippage showing secondary retouch which resulted from either knapping or usage. These tools represent the third most frequent artifacts with 1,147 examples. All are unifacially worked and every flake type has been utilized. Retouch ranges from large, well-defined flake scars, to small, almost undetectable chipping. A hand lens was required to recognize many of these implements, and no doubt many retouched flakes in the collection were missed. Large decortication hard hammer flakes were utilized as well as small flat and soft hammer flakes. It was on the latter flakes that the delicate, minuscule retouch was most frequently found. Without hafting it is inconceivable that these retouched flakes could have been used. Microscopic examination revealed a similar type of fracture pattern as found on scrapers. As with scrapers, chert is the dominant material with very few quartzite specimens. Much of this may be due to the difficulty in detecting small chippage on quartzite. The length of the retouched surface varies from about 2 centimeters to less than 1 centimeter. Because of the range in sizes and forms of these tools no measurements were made, and no attempt was made to devise a typology. Photographs of about twenty retouched flakes were taken, but the retouch could not be sufficiently reproduced to serve as an illustrative example.

Net Sinkers

Net sinkers are found over a wide geographical area with a variety of shapes and sizes. Those recovered from Naomikong Point are flat, smooth stones, usually circular, elliptical, or rectangular in shape, and otherwise unmodified except for two opposing notches. The latter are either "U"- or "V"-shaped and are produced by chipping as opposed to grinding. A total of 296 specimens comprise the assemblage. Measurements were made on 100 examples and the range and average of these measurements is given in Table 11. Plate XX *a-f* shows a sample from the collection.

The use of the net sinker by aboriginal populations occurs from Archaic to historic times, and there appears to have been

TABLE 11

RANGES AND AVERAGES OF ATTRIBUTES FROM A SAMPLING OF 100 NOTCHED STONE NET SINKERS

Attributes	Range	Average
Length (cm.)[1]	12.0- 4.1	7.9
Width (cm.)[2]	10.5- 4.8	6.5
Thickness (cm.)[2]	6.5- 0.7	2.1
Circumference (cm.)	40.9-19.0	25.6
Weight (gm.)	331- 0.7	165
Notch width (cm.)	3.3- 0.7	1.6
Notch depth (cm.)	0.6- 0.1	0.3

[1]Measured as the distance between the notches.
[2]Measured at L/2.

very little change in the nature of the artifact throughout this period. It has therefore been assumed that the function of these stones has remained constant through time. Such an assumption obliterates alternative possible uses, and also forces the interpretation of fishing activity. Most likely this is an accurate assumption, but alternative functional interpretations should be kept in mind. These might include bolas or use of weights on nets for trapping birds. The role of the net sinker in site interpretation is important, and a further elaboration on this subject will be presented in the next chapter.

Hammerstones

Compared with net sinkers, hammerstones are rare at Naomikong Point; only 32 are present. They occur throughout the site and are not concentrated in one locality. The size range is anywhere from a maximum length of 5 to 12 cms. with weights varying from 200 to 700 gms. Battering is usually confined to one end of the stone and in only one case is there wear around the entire circumference. Beach pebbles, of which there is an infinite supply, appear to have been utilized. Plate XX *h, i* illustrate two typical specimens from the site.

Celts and Pestles

Because there are so few of these classes of artifacts they have been lumped together. Five possible pestles and three celts were recovered from the site. The pestle identification is somewhat tenuous since only one complete example is present and the form is rather amorphous. This specimen is illustrated in

Plate XX*j*. The status of celts is similar to that of pestles since only one complete example is represented. This particular artifact is unfinished, and manufacturing terminated with the roughened shape. If this particular piece was ever utilized it cannot be detected from the artifact. The length is 18 cms. and the weight is slightly over 1 kg. Plate XX*g* illustrates this artifact.

COPPER

This section includes both copper artifacts and unmodified copper chunks. The latter should not be confused with raw copper ore, but it is copper that has been pounded into amorphous pieces. Some of these are no doubt badly oxidized artifacts whose form has been destroyed. Others are probably copper "blanks," that is, aboriginal ingots which would later be fashioned into an artifact. A total of 118 such pieces of copper are present, and these range from lengths of 1 to 4 cms.

Copper artifacts are mostly long, thin bipointed objects which were probably used as awls. These artifacts are represented by 33 examples ranging in length from 2 to 14 cms. Plate XXI*a* illustrates some of these items and Table 12 provides measurements. Unlike other artifact classes that are more or less evenly distributed over the site, copper occurs in concentrations. These groupings are not in caches but occur in areas of 10 to 15 square feet. Within a concentration both copper artifacts and unmodified pieces occur. While this might indicate an area of copper processing and artifact manufacture it is not reflected in the assemblage. As far as can be determined there are no partially-completed artifacts or pieces which indicate a transition from one stage of manufacture to another. This conclusion is of course affected by a large number of highly oxidized pieces, and this could produce a distorted picture.

In addition to awls, the copper assemblage includes: 9 beads (Plate XXI*b*), 3 cones (Plate XXI*c*), and two possible fish hooks. The identification of the latter was uncertain since it may be bent awls that are represented.

BONE TOOLS

Only one piece of worked bone was recovered during the two seasons of excavation and this was found in the surface-to-midden level. The artifact is incomplete and badly charred. It is

TABLE 12

METRIC ATTRIBUTES OF COPPER AWLS
(In Centimeters)

Catalogue Number	Length	Maximum Width	Maximum Thickness
72615	3.9	0.5	0.4
72615	2.9	0.5	0.3
72730	6.2	0.7	0.5
72735	4.0	1.0	0.7
72745	3.7	0.7	0.5
72757	9.2	0.4	0.3
72762	14.9	0.9	0.7
72803	4.6	0.7	0.4
72820	2.0	0.3	0.2
72820	7.4	0.5	0.5
72820	2.9	0.4	0.4
72830	4.0	0.6	0.5
72860	3.7	0.9	0.7
72866	4.0	0.6	0.2
72873	2.5	0.3	0.3
72885	2.6	0.4	0.3
72982	10.6	0.8	0.7
72995	5.6	0.8	0.4
73131	3.7	0.4	0.2
76066	2.8	0.8	0.7
76200	4.4	0.8	0.5
76249	5.1	0.6	0.4
76278	2.2	0.6	0.2
76291	5.2	0.4	0.3
76292	4.0	0.3	0.2
76298	4.0	0.6	0.4
76298	9.0	0.5	0.5
76332	4.5	0.4	0.2
76339	7.1	0.6	0.3
76373	2.1	0.4	0.7
76378	8.6	0.2	0.2
76378	3.2	0.8	0.2
76526	5.1	1.2	0.8

the tip of a hooked tool resembling a crochet needle. Most likely it is the tip of a harpoon. The length is 2.5 centimeters and the average diameter is 0.9 cm. No identification of the bone is possible other than to classify it as mammal. The artifact is illustrated in Plate XXI*d*.

FAUNAL REMAINS

Fauna from Naomikong Point can be divided into two groups. The first is an assortment of bone from the surface-to-midden level consisting of cow and deer, but predominantly beaver. This material was assignable to the historic occupations and perhaps the Late Woodland occupation. The second group of faunal remains consisted of calcined bone from the midden level. In order to restrict the faunal analysis to the aboriginal occupation, the bone in the first group was eliminated from the sample. Since there was some intrusion of this material into the midden it was impossible to segregate the historic from the prehistoric component. The calcined bone, being almost entirely confined to the midden, was considered for analysis.

Since bone reduced to a calcined condition is almost always fragmentary there were certain difficulties inherent in the bone analysis. First of all, no species or genera identifications were attempted. Three categories of bone presented themselves as being the most effective means of treating the particular sample. These categories were: mammal, fish, and unidentifiable. The last group consisted of the smallest fragmentary pieces and probably includes bird and turtle, of which there were otherwise no examples. Calcined bone in each of these categories was separated and weighed. The sample consisted of 1,127 grams of bone which represent 809 grams of mammal, 53 grams of fish, and 365 grams of unidentified bone. Since fish bone is rather diagnostic, there is some degree of certainty that the latter comprises only a small part of the unidentified category. It is interesting to note that although the large number of net sinkers imply a fishing site, the calcined bone data show mammal bone dominating by a ratio of 15 to 1.

A series of 25 soil pH tests were conducted for various portions of the site. The results indicated a range from an acid soil of pH 4.3 to a basic soil of pH 8.3. Concentrations of bone therefore may actually reflect soil conditions and not aboriginal activities.

HUMAN BURIALS

Although the heading Human Burials is used it is somewhat misleading. Unit 490 E 375 yielded one adult female skull minus the mandible. The area surrounding the skull was carefully examined and no trace of a pit outline could be determined.

Furthermore there was no associated material of any kind. The skull was found at the bottom of the midden, skull cap upwards, resting on sterile sand. The lack of associations and pit outline is puzzling and no interpretation of this "burial" will be attempted.

IV

INTERPRETATION OF ARCHAEOLOGICAL MATERIALS

INTRODUCTION

THE preceding chapter dealt with a description of the material inventory from Naomikong Point. Typologies were established for various artifact categories and these were supplemented with counts and artifact measurements. The purpose of the present chapter is to interpret these data. In order to accomplish this goal two statistical techniques will be employed, the chi-square test and the product-moment correlation coefficient. The distribution of the frequencies of artifact classes, per 5- by 5-foot excavation unit, will also be examined for the entire site. From this type of analysis inferences will be sought that relate to the dimensions of time, space, and culture. The former will point to those items in the culture in which a change through time is suspected. This can relate to either artifact or non-artifact changes. Spatial inferences attempt to delineate task-specific areas within the site. These will tie in with cultural inferences which relate to the nature of the social groupings. A further cultural inference dealing with "accepted" styles of ceramic decoration will be attempted.

There is a fundamental assumption in dealing with pottery that a vessel reflects the preconceived standards of the potter, and in general, these standards are much the same as those of the other potters in the society, or culture. In attempting to deal with this concept the archaeologist has the word "mode" in his vocabulary. According to Rouse (1960), a mode is:

> . . . any standard, concept, or custom which governs the behavior of the artisans of a community, which they hand down from generation to generation, and which may spread from community to community over considerable distances.

One deduces the ceramic modes of a culture through attributes. Attributes can be thought of as the lowest common denominators, or elements, which comprise the vessel as a whole, and include such items as temper, rim profile, bosses, etc. As Rouse (1960: 313) points out,

Not all the attributes of the artifact are indicative of modes. Some attributes will instead express personal idiosyncracies of the artisans.

The problem is to devise some method which will allow modes to be predicted from the totality of attributes. A statistical approach has been selected as a means of inferring modes and has been applied to eight attribute classes of the Naomikong Point ceramics: (1) rim profile, (2) major decorative style, (3) interior decoration, (4) rim decorative style, (5) lip decoration, (6) punctations, (7) bosses, and (8) drag stamping. These are the same attributes which were considered in Tables 4, 5, and 6.

MODAL ANALYSIS

The statistical test applied to the attribute frequencies is the chi-square test. This is a well known means of determining whether or not the frequencies obtained from observations differ significantly from the expected frequencies, given certain theoretical assumptions. A relatively large sample size is required, and it is assumed that there is a random sample. It is also necessary to establish a hypothesis pertaining to the relationship between the items being tested. The aim of this procedure, as it is applied to ceramic attributes, is to establish modes. In this study a null hypothesis has been made that has no relationship between any of the attributes. All those attributes which are not mutually exclusive will be considered in pairs of two, and subjected to the chi-square test. It should be noted from Tables 4, 5, and 6 that certain classes of attributes are mutually exclusive, such as the three for rim profile and the four attributes for both body and rim decoration. Naturally the attributes within each of these groups will not be tested among themselves. In some studies the main purpose of the chi-square test is to lump attributes and define types. In this case it is assumed that the typologies are correct, and the purpose is to determine the principal attributes, or modes. Each of the three types, Laurel Pseudo-scallop Shell, Laurel Pseudo-scallop Shell Naomikong Point variety, and Laurel Linear Stamp were examined separately and the attributes for each vessel were recorded. This gives the observed frequencies. The next step is to compute the expected frequencies. It was mentioned earlier that one of the initial conditions for the chi-square test is that a large sample size N is used. The question naturally arises as to how large is large? Blalock (1960:220) states that one means of deciding if N is of sufficient magnitude is to look at the expected frequencies in each cell. Should one of the expected frequencies be in the neighborhood of five or less, the number N is too small. When this situation arises it does not necessarily negate the chi-square test. A modification of the observed values, known as a correction for continuity, can be made by adding .5 to one observed frequency and subtracting .5 from the other. The net result of this manipulation is to reduce the magnitude of chi square, thus increasing the probability that the null hypothesis is correct.

There is an underlying assumption in this analysis that the most important mode is the tool type producing the decoration, for this is the attribute used for defining types. If it is assumed that the types are valid, the chi-square test is one way of determining which secondary attributes are also modes. With an alternately-notched stick, what are the culturally prescribed ways of decorating a pot? Are these ways the same or different for different types of pottery? These are a few of the kinds of questions that it is hoped a chi-square test can answer. In those cases where there is an expected frequency of five or less a correction for continuity will be made. Finally, in order to be somewhat confident in the interpretations derived from these tests, a significance level of 0.05 will be used. For tests having one degree of freedom, which is the case at hand, a chi-square value of 3.84 gives the desired level of significance.

For each of the three ceramic types being considered a total of 104 two by two chi-square tests were performed. The majority of the results indicate an attribute association that could be expected to occur by chance alone. Rather than present the results from 312 chi-square tests, only those with a significance of 0.05 or less will be considered. These are given in Appendix I. A summary of the results of the chi-square tests for each ceramic type will be given in a table and will accompany the discussion of these results. Table 13 presents the relevant chi-square data for Laurel Pseudo-scallop Shell.

The preceding chi-square tables indicate that there are 14 pairs of attributes which have a probability of less than 5 percent of occurring together by chance. There seems to exist many possible mode combinations which center around body and rim decoration. It should be remembered that the use of the term body decoration does not apply to the entire vessel but only to the upper one-half to one-third of the vessel. The remainder of the vessel is undecorated. Body decoration consisting of horizontal and oblique rows of parallel lines are dominant modes; with a number of accepted complementary decorative techniques.

TABLE 13

LAUREL PSEUDO-SCALLOP SHELL: SIGNIFICANT ATTRIBUTE ASSOCIATIONS WITH CHI-SQUARE VALUES AND PROBABILITY FACTORS

Test	Chi Square	Probability Factor
Attributes With Significant Positive Associations		
Straight rim/punctations	4.15	.05
Horizontal body decoration/vertical rim decoration	18.96	.001
Horizontal body decoration/oblique rim decoration	17.28	.001
Horizontal body decoration/bossing	7.77	.01
Oblique body decoration/rim and body decorated alike	29.71	.001
Oblique body decoration/punctations	15.96	.001
Rim and body decorated alike/punctations	4.96	.05
Vertical rim decoration/bossing	6.74	.01
Attributes With Significant Negative Associations		
Horizontal body decorations/rim and body decorated alike	52.17	.001
Horizontal body decorations/punctations	11.76	.001
Oblique body decoration/vertical rim decoration	14.10	.001
Oblique body decoration/oblique rim decoration	8.19	.01
Oblique body decoration/bossing	7.08	.01
Rim and body decorated alike/bossing	5.59	.02

The chi-square results indicate the presence of several decorative treatments. First, there is a tendency for oblique body decorations carried all the way to the lip of the vessel to be associated with a row of circular punctates encircling the rim. A second tendency is for horizontal body decorations to occur with an obliquely decorated rim. A variation on this pattern is the occurrence of horizontal body decoration with a vertically decorated rim, and bossing. Finally, straight rim profiles tend to be associated with punctations. In each of these cases a concern for rim decoration is seen. The rim is either set-off from the body decoration by changing the angle of decoration, or by using punctations. In the second case discussed two rim modes were employed.

Stoltman (1962:87-88) presents the results obtained from a similar study performed on Laurel pottery from Minnesota. Using chi-square tests Stoltman found that decorated lips and pseudo-scallop shell decoration occur together more frequently than expected by chance alone. The association of circular punctates with pseudo-scallop shell decoration appeared to be random. Thus the results obtained for Laurel Pseudo-scallop Shell from Naomikong Point differ from those obtained for similar pottery in Minnesota. Stoltman's study did not differentiate between various body and rim style decorations, and therefore no comparisons can be made of these attributes. Both studies suggested that there was no preferential association between pseudo-scallop shell decoration and bossing or drag-stamping.

Wright's (1967) data for Ontario Laurel fits nicely into the picture outlined here. Although the data are treated in a slightly different way and there are no chi-square tests, it is still possible to extract comparable information. At the Heron Bay, Pelican Falls, and Long Sault sites, the most frequent decorative motif on pseudo-scallop shell rim sherds was one row of oblique or vertical lines above horizontal lines. These are two of the attribute combinations which the chi-square test showed to be significant. The data for Ontario Laurel also indicates that on pseudo-scallop shell rim sherds, exterior punctations were more frequently present than absent. No data was available correlating punctations with body and rim treatment.

Chi-square data for attribute pairs of Laurel Pseudo-scallop Shell Naomikong Point variety are presented in Table 14.

The chi-square results show a marked difference in preferred attribute associations from those revealed for Laurel

TABLE 14

LAUREL PSEUDO-SCALLOP SHELL—NAOMIKONG POINT VARIETY: SIGNIFICANT ATTRIBUTE ASSOCIATIONS WITH CHI-SQUARE VALUES AND PROBABILITY FACTORS

Test	Chi Square	Probability Factors
Attributes With Significant Positive Associations		
Straight rim/interior decoration	7.75	.01
Straight rim/drag stamp	4.53	.05
Interior decoration/lip decoration	11.14	.001
Interior decoration/punctations	9.00	.01
Attributes With Significant Negative Associations		
Outsloping rim/interior decoration	5.97	.02
Outsloping rim/drag stamp	5.25	.05
Vertical body decoration/lip decoration	7.62	.01

Pseudo-scallop Shell. This may enforce the validity of establishing a variety of the latter type. Four attributes show a tendency to occur together in pairs and three of these involve interior rim decoration. The latter tends to associate with either straight rim profiles, lip decoration, or punctations. There is also a tendency for straight rims to occur with drag-stamped body decoration. It is interesting to note that while straight rims associate positively with either interior decoration or drag-stamping, outsloping rims show a strong tendency to avoid these two attributes. There seems to be practically no similarity in the modes established for this type and those found for Laurel Pseudo-scallop Shell. Both share the common mode of straight rim profile, however the Naomikong Point variety of Laurel Pseudo-scallop Shell shows a tendency for this mode to associate with drag-stamping rather than with punctations.

Since Stoltman (1962) does not recognize the type defined here as the Naomikong Point variety of Laurel Pseudo-scallop Shell it is difficult to make comparisons with his data. Stoltman's discussion on internal rim decoration (1962:62) is interesting and deserves some mention. In the Minnesota sample only one percent of the total number of rim sherds showed internal decoration. The conclusion is that this attribute probably represents idiosyncratic behavior, and therefore cannot be considered a mode. Data from Ontario Laurel sites (Wright, 1967) parallel the findings from Minnesota concerning internal decoration. Since the chi-square tests shown in Table 14 indicate just the opposite, it is interesting to speculate that perhaps there are spatial variations in Laurel ceramics. A range of usable attributes may be at the disposal of potters but those accepted as modes may vary geographically.

The results obtained from the chi-square tests on the type Laurel Linear Stamp are summarized in Table 15. This type reflects a set of modes which is different from the two previous types examined. Four pairs of attributes comprise the modes: straight rim profile with punctations, oblique body decoration carried to the lip of the vessel, oblique body decoration applied with a drag-stamped technique, and no body decoration with an obliquely decorated rim. The first two decorative styles are also modes shared with Laurel Pseudo-scallop Shell. The only mode crosscutting all three ceramic types is punctation. Stoltman (1962:91) in his analysis of Laurel Linear Stamp found that circular punctation could not be considered a mode, and thus another difference between Minnesota and Naomikong Point Laurel exists. It was mentioned in the above reference that Laurel

TABLE 15

LAUREL LINEAR STAMP: SIGNIFICANT ATTRIBUTE ASSOCIATIONS WITH CHI-SQUARE VALUES AND PROBABILITY FACTORS

Test	Chi Square	Probability Factors
Attributes With Significant Positive Associations		
Straight rim/punctations	5.64	.02
Oblique body decoration/rim and body decorated alike.	16.58	.001
Oblique body decoration/drag stamp	8.40	.01
Plain body/oblique rim decoration.	45.00	.001
Attributes With Significant Negative Associations		
Outsloping rim/punctations	4.54	.05
Oblique body decoration/oblique rim decoration. . . .	40.85	.001

Linear Stamp showed a genetic relationship to Laurel Push-and-pull. Since in the Naomikong Point ceramic analysis drag-stamping was not considered to be a defining criterion for a type, there is a deviation from Stoltman's typology. It is interesting to note, however, that drag-stamping appears as a mode for the type Laurel Linear Stamp in the Naomikong Point analysis.

The results of the chi-square tests have been to establish a set of modes for three Laurel pottery types. Each type appears to have a distinctive set of modes, although all share in the same general pool of attributes. From a modal point of view Laurel Pseudo-scallop Shell and Laurel Linear Stamp seem to be the most closely related since both share certain modes. Laurel Pseudo-scallop Shell Naomikong Point variety does not share any modal pairs with the latter two types. The only elements shared by all three types are punctations and a straight rim profile.

CERAMIC INTERPRETATION

The results of the chi-square tests indicate that each of the three ceramic types examined display a somewhat distinctive set of modes. In the case of the two Laurel Pseudo-scallop Shell types the apparently different set of modes associated with each type is one step in establishing the validity of a separate classification. At the beginning of this section three types of archaeological interpretation were discussed. The chi-square results will now be considered in terms of the dimensions of time, space, and culture. In defining modes the cultural aspect of the data has been considered. It is logical to ask if these modes have temporal or spatial significance. They may indicate changes through time of culturally accepted attributes or attribute clusters. The likelihood also exists that these types which have been examined are the products of distinct social groups within the society. Another alternative is that they reflect functional differences. In order to assess these various possibilities the distribution of the three types, Laurel Pseudo-scallop Shell, the Naomikong Point variety of the latter, and Laurel Linear Stamp were examined. The other Laurel types in the collection have been omitted from consideration due to their relatively small number.

The distribution of each of the types mentioned above was plotted according to the number of vessels per major excavation unit. Since some of these units yielded relatively few vessels they were lumped with other units. The 1966 Beach Trench was included with unit A, the 1965 Test Trench with unit B, and the 1967 Beach Trench with unit D. The midden discontinuity in the 5- by 60-foot trench discussed in the section on stratigraphy was taken into consideration in plotting the distribution of pottery types. The latter trench was divided into two parts; one section lying east of the midden discontinuity and the other lying to the west. The distribution of the ceramic types by number of vessels is given in Table 16. Mackinac ware is also shown in this table to indicate the distribution of a Late Woodland type relative to the three Laurel types.

The picture which emerges from Table 16 is hardly the expected one. Laurel Pseudo-scallop Shell and its variety show a very similar distribution over the site. If the midden discontinuity is used to divide the site, approximately 93 percent of the vessels of both types lie to the east of the discontinuity. Laurel Linear Stamp vessels show an entirely different distribution with only 64 percent of the vessels found to the east of the midden discontinuity. In fact, the Laurel Linear Stamp distribution approximates the Mackinac ware distribution more closely than the distribution of the two other Laurel types. A comparison of the three Laurel types does not seem to indicate that functional differences are present. Vessels are all approximately the same size and other than the use of a dentate or simple tool, all three share the same basic set of decorative attributes. If it is assumed that these three types are synchronic and their distribution reflects different cultural groups then a somewhat more mutually

TABLE 16

SPACIAL DISTRIBUTION OF CERAMIC VESSELS AT THE NAOMIKONG POINT SITE

Type	5 by 30	Units						
		A (1)	B (2)	C	5 by 60 (3)	5 by 60 (4)	D (5)	E
Laurel Pseudo-scallop Shell .	10	27	32	12	6	...	6	...
Laurel Pseudo-scallop Shell - Naomikong Point Variety. .	7	24	18	7	2	1	2	1
Laurel Linear Stamp	12	23	7	12	3	7	22	3
Mackinac ware	...	20	4	6	1	2	8	10

	Total	Number East of Break	Percent	Number West of Break	Percent	Chi Square	Probability
Laurel Pseudo-scallop Shell .	93	87 (56.7)*	93.3	6 (36.3)	6.7	41.5	.001
Laurel Pseudo-scallop Shell - Naomikong Point Variety. .	62	58 (37.8)	93.5	4 (24.2)	6.5	27.6	.001
Laurel Linear Stamp	89	57 (54.3)	64.1	32 (34.7)	35.9	0.41	.50
Mackinac ware	51	31 (31.1)	60.8	20 (19.9)	39.2	...	.97

Note: (1) includes 1966 Beach Trench
(2) includes 1965 Test Trench
(3) units east of the discontinuity
(4) units west of the discontinuity
(5) includes 1967 Beach Trench
* expected frequencies

exclusive spatial distribution might be expected. At least the observed distribution would not be expected. Of the total 110 5- by 5-foot units excavated, 67 are to the east of the midden discontinuity. This represents 61 percent of the site. If a uniform distribution of pottery types over the site is assumed, then approximately 54 Laurel Linear Stamp vessels would be expected to the east of the discontinuity and 35 to the west. The observed frequencies are 57 and 32 respectively. A chi-square value of 0.41 is obtained when these figures are tested. For one degree of freedom, this gives a probability value of 0.5. The observed distribution of Mackinac ware deviates from the expected by only one-tenth, giving a chi-square value of nearly zero. Laurel Pseudo-scallop Shell and the Naomikong Point variety of this type show an entirely different distribution. Of the 145 vessels of both types only 10 occur to the west of the midden discontinuity. If these vessels were uniformly distributed about the discontinuity, as Laurel Linear Stamp and Mackinac ware appear to be, then approximately 60 vessels would be expected to the west of the discontinuity. A chi-square test run on these figures gives a value of 80. Obviously this is highly significant.

Certain assumptions were used in arriving at these results: first, that the ceramic typologies are valid, second, that the midden discontinuity is a valid point for dividing the site, and third, that a uniform distribution of ceramics is on either side of this discontinuity. Given these assumptions the following hypothesis is proposed; at the Naomikong Point site, dentate tool-decorated pottery and simple tool-decorated pottery represent chronologically different periods within the Laurel tradition, dentate tool decoration being earlier than simple tool decoration. This last statement is based on the similarity in distribution of Laurel Linear Stamp and Mackinac ware. It is also interesting to note that two associated modes for Laurel Linear Stamp (undecorated body and oblique rim decoration) are two commonly associated attributes of Mackinac ware. In the latter, the rim decoration may not always be oblique, but the same basic pattern of confining decoration to the rim is followed.

The transition from dentate to simple tool-decorated pottery is not seen as an abrupt change, but as slowly changing relative frequency differences through time. Throughout this period the preference for making vessels with straight rims and adding a single row of circular punctates around the rim was maintained.

SPATIAL ANALYSIS OF ARCHAEOLOGICAL MATERIALS

Thus far in this section the modal analysis of three ceramic types has attempted to probe the cultural dimension of the data, and a hypothesis has been postulated which deals with the dimension of time. A spatial analysis of all archaeological material from the site will now be attempted. The goal of this analysis is to determine if there is a tendency for certain classes of artifacts and/or non-artifacts to be associated together. From this information it may be possible to make inferences relating to the various activities which were carried out at the site, and perhaps even be able to delineate the areas where they were taking place. In order to achieve this goal a product-moment correlation analysis was performed on the data. This test produces a coefficient that is a measure of the linear relationship between two items. The value of the coefficient (designated by the letter r) can range from 1.0 to -1.0, the former relating to a perfect positive relationship and the latter to a perfect negative one.

In the introductory remarks of Part II a statement was made that the method of collection of archaeological data is influenced by the questions the archaeologist asks. The problem of defining activity areas within a site requires that there be spatial control over the data. A unit size of 5 by 5 feet was selected since it was sufficiently small to give this control, yet at the same time had the potential of producing a large quantity of material. It was therefore considered ideal for obtaining data which could be applied to a product-moment correlation. This aside was inserted to illustrate that the excavation techniques were dictated by the nature of the problem and the type of analysis used.

For each of the 110 5- by 5-foot units a total of 27 variables were considered. These included: counts on all chippage and core categories and the total number of each, the total weight of chippage, the total number of sherds (the number greater than one inch and less than one inch and the weight of the latter), the number of projectile points, scrapers, preforms, and worked flakes, the number of net sinkers, hammerstones, copper awls, and the total number of vessels of each of the types shown in Table 16. The total number of pieces of copper was considered, as well as the number and weight of charred bone and the weight of fire-cracked rock. Special categories of data included the number of scrapers made on decortication flakes, the number of quartzite flakes and artifacts, and the number of flakes showing heat action.

Correlation coefficients were computed for all possible pairs of the above categories using an IBM 7090 computer. A total of 8 runs was made by considering the site in various sections. These were: the total site, that portion of the site to the east of the midden discontinuity, that portion to the west, and each of the 5 20- by 20-foot units. The correlation coefficients obtained for these various divisions of the site ranged continuously from 0.99 to -0.43. Table 17 gives the distribution of the correlation coefficients, within one-tenth unit intervals, for each test that was run.

For the total site (110 units) any correlation coefficient of 0.24 or greater is statistically significant at the 0.01 level. One hundred and seventy-eight correlation coefficients, out of a total of 351, were within this range. These coefficients indicated an intercorrelation among sherds, scrapers, worked flakes, all chippage categories, bipolar and block cores, copper awls and fragments, and heat-treated flakes. With this degree of intercorrelation no task-specific areas within the site could be identified. All activities appear to be taking place together.

If the 0.05 level of significance is considered, then all coefficients of 0.18 and greater are statistically significant. The same artifactual and non-artifactual material which correlated at the 0.01 level are even more highly intercorrelated. In this case 178 correlation coefficients are involved.

The correlation coefficients obtained by dividing the site at the midden discontinuity reveal the same type of situation found for the total site. East of the midden discontinuity there are 67 5- by 5-foot units. In this case any correlation coefficient of 0.32 or greater is statistically significant at the 0.01 level. A total of 165 correlation coefficients (out of 351) were within this range. These showed the same types of relationships that were found for the total site. For the 0.05 level, coefficients of 0.24 or greater are statistically significant and a total of 204 coefficients were within this range. West of the midden discontinuity there are 43 5- by 5-foot units and coefficients of 0.38 or greater are statistically significant at the 0.01 level. There were 121 coefficients in this category and they pertained to the same items which have been mentioned for the total site and that portion of the site east of the midden discontinuity. At the 0.05 level, coefficients of 0.29 and greater are statistically significant and 201 are within this range.

For product-moment tests run on the 5 20- by 20-foot units, correlation coefficients of 0.59 and greater are statistically significant at the 0.01 level. The number of statistically significant

TABLE 17

CORRELATION COEFFICIENTS

Range of Correlation Coefficients	Total Site (110)*	East of Discontinuity	West of Discontinuity	A (16)*	B (16)	C (16)	D (16)	E (16)
-.50 to -.41	...	...	...	...	...	2	...	7
-.40 to -.31	...	...	...	3	...	8	8	11
-.30 to -.21	...	...	4	11	9	14	22	26
-.20 to -.11	...	2	21	24	18	44	30	44
-.10 to -.01	35	22	43	18	22	37	31	33
.00	7	4	4	2	...	3	4	54
.01 to .09	55	51	43	37	26	34	39	22
.10 to .19	60	58	41	46	26	53	38	26
.20 to .29	53	50	44	49	30	32	36	38
.30 to .39	41	52	38	43	41	41	31	27
.40 to .49	24	38	22	36	26	28	41	12
.50 to .59	33	29	32	37	26	18	27	20
.60 to .69	26	24	22	24	29	20	24	10
.70 to .79	11	16	25	15	28	13	16	11
.80 to .89	3	3	11	4	36	3	4	8
.90 to .99	1	3	1	2	34	1	...	2

*Number of 5 by 5 ft. units included in major unit.

coefficients for units A, B, C, D, and E are respectively: 47, 128, 48, 45, and 31. With the exception of unit B, most statistically significant correlation coefficients pertain to scrapers, worked flakes, and chippage categories. Unit B will be discussed later. The number of statistically significant coefficients at the 0.05 level (r = 0.47) for units A, B, C, D, and E are respectively: 98, 256, 76, 78, and 62.

Although it is difficult to remember this large array of numbers, they all basically reveal the same picture. For units A, C, D, and E there is an intercorrelation between chippage categories, scrapers, and worked flakes. As larger areas of the site were considered (with the exception of unit B), stronger intercorrelations resulted among these categories as well as sherds, copper, and cores. In general, by examining the statistically significant correlation coefficients from eight separate tests there is very little information that can be derived. Activities are either not confined to sections of the site, or continuous seasonal habitation of the site has thoroughly mixed artifactual and non-artifactual material.

In order to extract some meaning from the product-moment test, the higher correlation coefficients were examined. Since unit B displayed the greatest number of statistically significant coefficients of all the 20- by 20-foot units it was reexamined. An increase in the number of coefficients in the last two intervals (see Table 17) was noted. A total of 70 coefficients of .80 and greater strongly intercorrelate the following categories; sherds, scrapers, worked flakes, all chippage categories, and heat-treated flakes. There is also a high degree of intercorrelation between quartzite, flat and block flakes, weight of calcined bone, and the number of pieces of unworked copper.

Since there was such a large number of correlation coefficients of 0.80 and greater in unit B, the other tests were examined to see how they respond at this level. Appendix II gives the correlation coefficients of .80 and greater for each test. Unit B is not listed in Appendix II because of the large number of coefficients involved.

Total Site

Only four correlation coefficients of 0.80 or greater were obtained for the total site and all relate to the total chippage count. Correlation coefficients of .81, .83, .88, and .93 correspond respectively to the total chippage count versus total number of scrapers, number of decortication flakes, number of block flakes, and number of flat flakes.

East of Midden Discontinuity

The correlation coefficients of .80 or greater reflect the same situation as seen for the total site. The correlation coefficients of .80, .80, .93, and .95 correspond respectively to the total chippage count versus the total number of scrapers, number of decortication flakes, number of flat flakes, and number of block flakes. A coefficient of .90 was obtained for block flakes versus flat flakes and .82 for scrapers versus worked flakes.

West of Midden Discontinuity

The correlation coefficients of .80 and greater for this portion of the site show a wider range of relationships. Scrapers correlate with sherds (r = .88), total chippage (r = .83), decortication flakes (r = .83), block flakes (r = .85), and flat flakes (r = .93). Bipolar cores, flakes of bifacial retouch, heat-treated flakes, copper and hard hammer flakes also enter the picture as seen in Appendix II.

20- by 20-Foot Units

Figure 4 (p. 18) should be referred to for the various 20- by 20-foot unit designations. Units A, B, and C are continguous units located to the east of the midden discontinuity. Unit A has six correlation coefficients of .80 or greater; five of these relate to correlations between chippage categories. The four correlation coefficients (.80 and greater) for unit C, are almost identical to unit A. All coefficients correlate chippage categories, and three of them are also in unit A.

Units D and E do not reflect the same groupings of correlation coefficients as found in units A and C. In unit D the four correlation coefficients of .80 and greater correlate: sherds and scrapers (r = .87), total number of chippage and flat flakes (r = .87), total pieces of copper and decortication flakes (r = .84), and the weight of calcined bone and block flakes (r = .82). Ten correlation coefficients (.80 and greater) are present in unit E. Three of these relate to quartzite, quartzite flakes and decortication flakes (r = .83), quartzite flakes and total chippage (r = .82), and quartzite artifacts and hard hammer flakes (r = .80). Unit E is unique in that it is the only unit which has high correlation coefficients relating to preforms preforms and sherds, (r = .90), and preforms and weight of calcined bone, (r = .83) and to quartzite chippage and artifacts. Since unit E yielded the largest proportion of Late Woodland sherds, quartzite and preforms may represent the Late Woodland occupation.

This concludes the discussion of the high (.80 and greater) correlation coefficients. The most unexpected observation was the large number of correlation coefficients of .80 and greater in unit B. The high degree of intercorrelation among all chippage types, heat-treated flakes, scrapers, and worked flakes indicates that this is a focal point of flint knapping and artifact manufacture. The fact that heat-treated flakes correlate with all types of chippage in the area of greatest workshop activity certainly implies that this was an essential step in working flint. The intercorrelation of all chippage types, scrapers, and worked flakes with the number of sherds, and pieces of copper may indicate that unit B was not restricted to knapping activities. If the post mold and feature distribution of units A, B, and C are considered (Figure 9, p. 27), some interesting speculations can be made. The greatest concentration of post molds and features occurs in units A and C, while only two post molds and one prehistoric feature (17-66) are located in unit B. Although no pattern is discernible from the post mold distribution in units A and C, it is apparent that in terms of the post molds, features, and similarity in correlation coefficients, that these units reflect a different activity pattern from that of unit B. The presence of post molds does not necessarily imply houses so units A and C cannot categorically be classed as dwelling areas. The interpretation of the pattern displayed by units A, B, and C is one of two social groupings, one occupying unit A and one unit C. The area in between, unit B, served as a common working area for both groups. The large number of intercorrelated items further suggests that possibly male and female activities were carried out in this area. The high correlation between the total number of sherds (female activity) and total chippage count (male activity), substantiates the suggestion that this activity area was not sexually segregated.

At first it may appear that a different situation exists in units A, B, and C than in units D and E, however, upon closer inspection these differences become smaller. The northern half of unit D yielded a relatively greater quantity of all classes of artifactual material than the southern half of the unit, and this closely parallels the relationship between unit B and units A and C. At this point Figure 9 should be referred to again and the post mold and feature distribution in units D and E noted. In this case the post molds and features are concentrated in the southern portion of unit D and the western portion of the 5- by 60-foot trench. This situation is interpreted as the same activity pattern as for units A, B, and C. The area around the post molds and features being one task-specific area with other activities carried on around the periphery. In this case all activity is being performed by one social group which may explain why there are fewer high correlations among the data as compared to unit B.

The activities taking place in unit D are probably closely linked to the western half of the 5- by 60-foot trench. It is interesting to note that associated with unit D, to the east, is Feature 9-67 which was interpreted as a refuse area. The only other feature of this kind is Feature 17-66 which is associated with the activity focal point in units A, B, and C. The contents of these features included practically an entire spectrum of artifactual and non-artifactual material. The fact that each is associated with a major center of activity may indicate that they served as refuse areas. Since a refuse pit might be expected to have a high correlation among its contents it is possible that the large number of intercorrelations for unit B all relate to refuse material. This does not appear to be the case since the area surrounding these features produced as much, if not more, material than the features.

One comment should be made regarding the pattern which has been established for unit B and the northern portion of unit D. These have been called workshop areas, however, they are not necessarily task-specific areas. Some of the same activities being performed in these areas were carried on elsewhere. It is the intensity of many classes of artifact and non-artifact materials in unit B and the northern half of unit D that sets them off as special areas.

SUBSISTENCE PATTERN

Within the cultural framework that has thus far been established, the subsistence economy will now be considered. The subsistence activities at Naomikong Point are extremely difficult to determine from the data. The only reliable faunal remains from the prehistoric midden are calcined bone, and these have been reduced to such a small size that they are unidentifiable other than the gross classification of mammal and fish. The former is represented by 809 grams while the latter consists of 53 grams. These weights convert to 94 percent mammal and 6 percent fish. This cannot be interpreted as an indication that 94 percent of the food was derived from mammal and the other

6 percent from fish. Such factors as food preparation and degree of preservation could affect these percentages. As a result there is very little archaeological data from which the subsistence pattern can be inferred. With the lack of empirical evidence it is necessary to turn to logical evidence. The proximity of the site to the lake suggests that fishing may have been a major source of food. The Whitefish Bay area was known historically as a good site for fishing, and in the journal of Lt. James Allen, a member of the Schoolcraft party, this location is cited as the only place where whitefish could be taken in the spring (Mason, 1958:166). Another historic reference (Pitezel, 1901:40) refers to Na-gah-ne-kong (Naomikong) as the best site in Tahquamenon Bay for catching whitefish. These two references indicate that the Naomikong Point site is in a favorable location for fishing as known in the historic period, and it is probably valid to extend this condition into the prehistoric era.

Many archaeologists would have arrived at this conclusion by considering the presence of 296 "net sinkers" as empirical evidence indicating fishing. The weakness in this reasoning is that it presupposes that the function of these artifacts is known. Rather than take this approach the presence of net sinkers will be used to support the position that Naomikong Point was a favorable location for fishing during Middle Woodland times.

None of the product-moment correlation coefficients indicated a significant relationship (r = .80) between net sinkers and any other items tested. One possible explanation is that net sinkers, other than occurring on nets, were not used with any other type of artifact. Their greatest concentration was in unit B where 99 were recovered. In the northern half of unit D, 33 were found while only 15 were recovered from the southern portion. The remainder of the net sinkers were distributed over the site as follows: unit A (16), unit C (25), unit E (38), 5- by 60-foot trench (33). A total of 9 net sinkers was recovered from the beach trenches and the 5- by 30-foot trench. The distribution of these artifacts, as well as all others, may give a hint as to the structure of the community. If the groups at the site were organized into a community-cooperating unit then some spatially distinct areas at the site might be expected. These might include a community cooking area, chipping area, and craft area. If the site were proportioned in this way it should have been detected by the product-moment test since some high negative coefficients would have resulted. The fact that there were very few negative coefficients and that these never were statistically significant suggests that this type of community pattern is absent. Therefore, rather than a community-wide cooperative fishing effort, it appears more likely that each household, or extended family, acted as an independent unit with net sinkers (or nets) kept in the vicinity of their living areas.

This type of fishing pattern parallels the Chippewa fishing practices described by Schoolcraft at Sault Ste. Marie in 1820 (Williams, 1953:103). Fish were taken by two men, one steering the canoe and the other catching fish with a scoop net. The fish were then cured by smoke drying and stored for future use. If this account is used as a model, the small amount of fish bone at Naomikong Point could indicate that fish were being dried and stored without being filleted. Perhaps during this period mammals were more frequently relied upon as food. The post molds and features in units A, C, and D may represent the smoking areas at the site. Since net sinkers are not used on scoop nets, either this technique of fishing was not used, or the functional interpretation of these artifacts is in error.

SETTLEMENT PATTERN

Data pertaining to most of the aspects of settlement pattern are absent. No information on house type or the relative position of structures could be determined. The only inference regarding settlement pattern that can be made relates to the seasonality of the occupation. This inference is relatively weak since it is derived from another inference, that the major subsistence economy is fishing. Historically, as cited in Allen's journal (Mason, 1958:166), the fishing season at Whitefish Bay is from the end of April to the end of June, and from the first part of October to mid-November. If fishing is the major activity at Naomikong Point, and if the historic information on fishing is valid for the Middle Woodland period, then these dates probably bracket the occupation periods of the site. An estimate of the population at the site at any one time is difficult to assess. The presence of Middle Woodland, Late Woodland, and Proto-Historic material indicates that the area was inhabited for a long period of time. A limited number of test pits showed that spatially the site was very large, and the excavations may have only tapped 1 percent of the site. It seems reasonable to assume that the Middle Woodland population at any one time would be composed of a minimum of fifteen persons representing maybe four lodges. It is certainly possible that this number was exceeded by an order of magnitude.

CONCLUSIONS

The analysis of the Laurel occupation at Naomikong Point has been approached in terms of the dimensions of time, space, and culture. The latter has received little attention from archaeologists working with Laurel material and therefore this dimension has been accented here. In terms of the Laurel culture as a whole, the dimensions of time and space will now be examined.

The Naomikong Point site is situated to the south and east of the major cultural development of Laurel, as it is presently known. The temporal relationship of the site with the rest of Laurel is unknown in terms of absolute dates. Four samples of charred "food" from the interior of vessels were submitted to the University of Michigan Radiocarbon Laboratory. Unfortunately, contamination and equipment failure plagued these samples, and only one date was obtained. The scrappings from a partially complete Laurel Pseudo-scallop shell Naomikong Point variety vessel (unit 525 E 525: midden level) produced a radiocarbon date of 1520 ± 400 B.C. or A.D. 430 (M-2055).

The dimensions of time, space, and culture will now be considered within the Naomikong Point site itself. A hypothesis was proposed based upon the modal analysis of three Laurel ceramic types and their distribution at the site. The nature of this hypothesis is that dentate and simple tool-decorated pottery represent a cultural change through time, and that the latter succeeds the former.

With the aid of product-moment correlation tests the relationship of artifact and non-artifact categories was examined. The following cultural picture emerged. Two relatively distinct activity areas are present at the site. The first area is associated with post molds and features and the by-products of flint working activities. This area is interpreted as an activity area of a single social unit which could be either the extended or nuclear family. The second area is always adjacent to the first and indicates that more diversified activities are being performed. This type of area is interpreted as a workshop area where both male and female activities are carried out. A large refuse pit is always associated with these areas and their contents include all categories of artifactual and non-artifactual material. Each social unit probably operated independently although in unit B two groups appear to have shared a common workshop area. The main activity at the site centered around fishing which was carried out independently by each group. The lack of a pattern to the post mold distribution suggests that these could perhaps represent the remains of drying racks rather than dwellings. The fires used for this purpose would be kept smothered so they would smoke and thus the common red oxidized sands associated with fire pits were absent. Some features associated with the post molds may be such fire pits.

Fishing was done on a seasonal basis in either the late spring or fall, or at both times. The groups probably returned to the site for many years and established themselves in approximately the same location they had occupied before. This is inferred from the random post mold pattern and the large quantity of workshop debris which seems unlikely to have accumulated in a single season's activities.

Local resources were utilized for stone tools. Beach pebbles served to fashion net sinkers, and locally derived cherts and quartzite were used for scrapers and projectile points. Naomikong Point provided one of the few sand beaches in the area, fish were plentiful, and stone material was available. All three factors probably played a role in the location of the settlement.

These groups were certainly not culturally isolated. The presence of obsidian from Wyoming, a Snyder's-like point possibly from the Illinois area, dentate pottery which reflects Hopewellian influence, a linear-stamped vessel almost identical to one from Summer Island in northern Lake Michigan, and pseudo-scallop shell decorated pottery which is found eastward to the Atlantic Coast all indicate that external influences were present. Whether these were via direct contact or through trade networks, a mechanism for the exchange of cultural ideas was present.

Since Laurel is spread over a large geographical area the degree of external influences may vary from site to site. This may produce internal variations in the culture, particularly in those cultural items like pottery where craft techniques can change without changing the function of the artifact. Items which bear on the exploitation of the environment, like scrapers, may be less susceptible to change. Although the temporal division of Laurel derived from the ceramic analysis is unproven, the presence of some Late Woodland material is unmistakable. The material from unit E is believed to be mostly Late Woodland derived. If the pottery and eight triangular projectile points were removed from the unit E collection the remaining material would appear homogeneous with the rest of the site.

The concluding portion of this discussion is permeated with the words "probable," and "seems." The analysis of the data indicates that something is happening. This "something" has been interpreted. The model which has been established is not the only one possible. It is believed to be the most accurate one, although others may be derived from the data. Hopefully the data have been presented so those who disagree with the present model can establish new ones. A comparison of other Laurel sites will be made in the next section where the model will be tested.

V

NORTHERN MIDDLE WOODLAND RELATIONSHIPS

INTRODUCTION

THE term "Middle Woodland" refers to that period of time between 200 B.C. and A.D. 400 when most of Eastern North America was dominated by the Hopewellian culture. In the Upper Great Lakes area, extending from Southern Manitoba to New York State, Middle Woodland cultures show a Hopewellian flavoring as well as a great deal of internal consistency. The term "Northern Middle Woodland" is applied to these cultures. Representative cultures of this group include; Laurel, North Bay, Saugeen, and Point Peninsula. Recognizing the similarities in these cultures Mason (1967:338) has grouped them under the heading "Northern Tier Middle Woodland," while Fitting (1965) has suggested the term "Lake Forest Middle Woodland." In this section the various Northern Middle Woodland cultures will be reviewed. Differences and similarities will be examined as well as the relationships that exist among them as a group. The model established for Naomikong Point will be applied specifically to the Laurel culture. Figure 12 is a map of the Northern Middle Woodland area. The major sites are located on this map and may be referred to throughout this discussion.

THE LAUREL CULTURE

The name, Laurel, was first used by Wilford (1941) to define a focus which applied to Middle Woodland burial mounds in northern Minnesota. This was established as the single focus of the Rainy River aspect, Lake Michigan phase of the Woodland pattern. The excavations upon which the focus was defined were carried out by Professor Lloyd A. Wilford between the years of 1933 and 1940. Four mounds were excavated during this period, Smith Mound 4, McKinstry Mounds 1 and 2, and the Pike Bay Mound. It is from the location of the Smith Mound group near Laurel, Minnesota that the focus derived its name. The artifactual material recovered in these excavations was all derived from mound fill

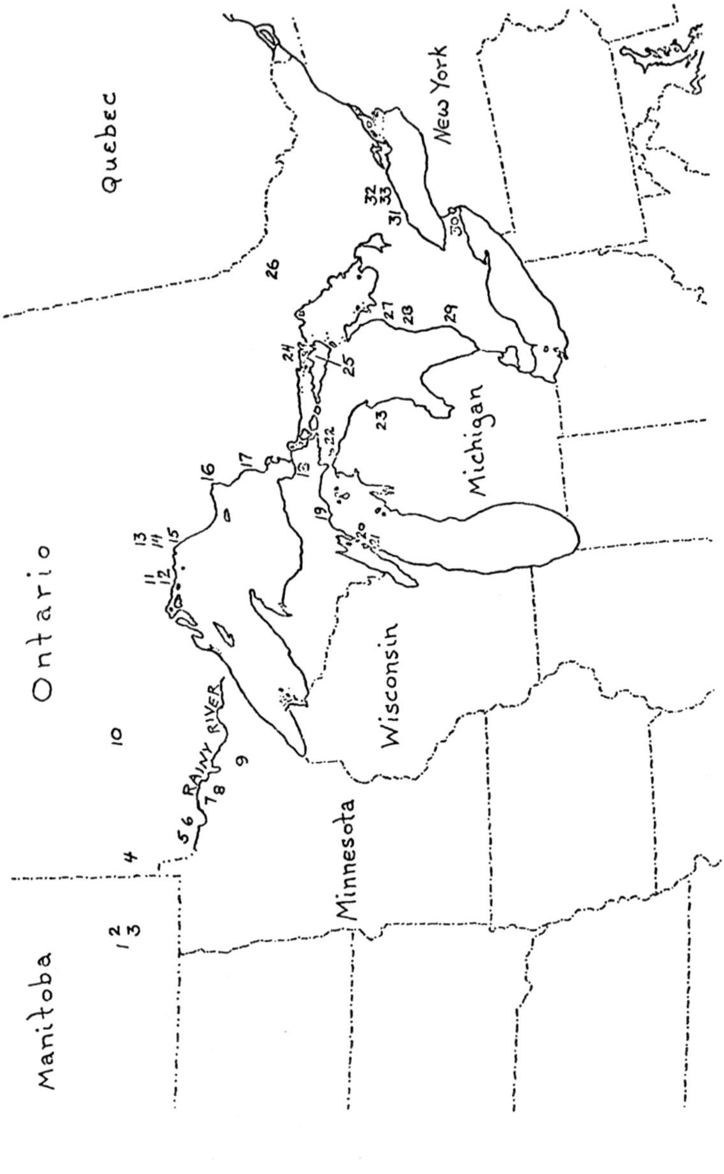

FIG. 12. Map of Northern Middle Woodland Sites. 1. Lockport, 2. Anderson, 3. Cemetery Point, 4. Swan Lake, 5. Hungry Hall, 6. Long Sault, 7. McKinstry, 8. Smith Mounds, 9. Pike Bay, 10. Pelican Falls, 11. Pays Platt, 12. Rossport, 13. Killala Lake, 14. Little Pic, 15. Heron Bay, 16. Michipicoten Harbor, 17. Sand River (Agawa Bay), 18. Naomikong Point, 19. Ekdahl-Goodreau, 20. Summer Island, 21. Porte des Morts and Mero, 22. Arrowhead Drive, 23. Goodwin-Gresham, 24. Killarney, 25. Sheguiandah, 26. Frank Bay, 27. Donaldson, 28 Inverheron, 29. Burley, 30. Newman, 31. Short, 32. Cameron's Point, 33. Serpent Mounds.

and most likely represented debris from a habitation area. Pot sherds were the most frequent artifact recovered from each mound, and all four mounds yielded over 16,000 sherds, as compared with only about 300 artifacts of stone, bone, copper, and shell. In general, the ceramics were characterized by a set of decorative attributes which consisted of a pseudo-scallop shell motif, dentate and linear stamping, both interior and exterior punctations which may or may not produce bosses, and a push-pull or drag-stamped method of application.

The burial mounds were approximately circular, and ranged from 50 to 84 feet in diameter and from 4.5 to 8.5 feet in height. They appear to have been constructed in several stages and were even utilized in Late Woodland times as evidenced by intrusive burials associated with Blackduck pottery. Laurel burial practices were characterized by secondary bundle burials and at the Smith Mound there was evidence of intentional tampering with the skull and long bones, probably for the extraction of the brains and marrow (Stoltman, 1962:10). Burial accompaniment was almost totally absent, the only exception being at the McKinstry Mound 1 where a necklace of 2,200 cut shell beads was found associated with two human vertebrae.

Thus the picture of Laurel in the 1940's was confined to the northern Minnesota area, and the defining criteria for the focus rested on ceramics and burial practices. In the early 1950's Richard MacNeish, working in southern Manitoba, excavated three sites which showed Laurel affinities. These were the Lockport, Cemetery Point, and Anderson sites. The Nutimik focus was established on the basis of material recovered from the first two sites, while material from the third site and Levels 9 and 10 at the Lockport site were used to establish the Anderson focus. The distinct stratigraphic separation of the two foci at the Lockport site indicated that Nutimik succeeded Anderson. Although temporally distinct, the ceramics of both are characterized by dentate body decorations and bossed and circular punctated rims. Additional characteristics of Nutimik ceramics include: incising and/or rocker-stamping, horizontal bands of vertical impressions (drag-stamping?), cord-wrapped-stick impressions, and cord-marked bodies (MacNeish, 1958:13-40). The diagnostic pseudo-scallop shell decoration of Minnesota Laurel sites is relatively scarce on Manitoba sites. No sherds of this type were recovered from the Anderson focus levels. The ceramic type Nutimik Oblique (MacNeish, 1958:150-51), which occurs almost exclusively in the Nutimik focus, includes sherds which today can be classified among the pseudo-scallop shell types. The exact number of these sherds included under the label Nutimik Oblique cannot be determined. Since the Nutimik focus levels yielded only 151 Nutimik Oblique sherds (or 18 percent of the total ceramic assemblage), that portion which is pseudo-scallop shell cannot be very large.

The lithic assemblages from the two foci were sparse. The Anderson focus was represented by 22 items, the two most frequent being scrapers and preforms which occurred in almost equal proportions. Of the 77 items from the Nutimik focus over half were scrapers.

The early 1960's saw a resurgence in the discovery of Laurel sites. A Laurel component belonging to the Anderson focus was identified at the stratified Pelican Narrows site in east central Saskatchewan (Brown, 1962:120). Northern Ontario entered the picture with the excavations of W. A. Kenyon (1960 and 1961) in the Rainy River area, and James V. Wright's work (1963 and 1967) along the north shore of Lake Superior. As a result of these works the geographical range of Laurel was extended to the eastern shore of Lake Superior, a distance of over 400 miles from the type sites on the Rainy River. The presence of burial mounds at the Hungry Hall site and Long Sault site, both on the Canadian side of the Rainy River, show a continuity with Minnesota Laurel. The ceramic assemblage from these sites was relatively small with 37 and 27 rim sherds in the Hungry Hall and Long Sault collections respectively. Pseudo-scallop shell decoration dominated the latter sample while dentate stamping was the most frequent decoration at the former site. Bossing was rare with one rim sherd from Hungry Hall and two rim sherds from Long Sault displaying this characteristic.

It is somewhat difficult to extract a lowest common denominator for the Rainy River Laurel sites unless it is the presence of burial mounds. The ceramic assemblage from each site seems to display distinctive characteristics. Pottery from the McKinstry 1 mound has a high incidence of pseudo-scallop shell decoration, whereas the Pike Bay site has a high frequency of linear and drag-stamping. The Smith Mounds, on the other hand, have a higher proportion of dentate stamping than any other decorative type (Stoltman, 1962:95-97). As already mentioned, the Hungry Hall and Long Sault sites displayed differences in the relative frequency of dentate stamping and pseudo-scallop shell decoration. At the present time Stoltman is reexamining Minnesota Laurel ceramics in terms of intrasite variation (personal communication).

Another common characteristic of Minnesota Laurel is the toggle head harpoon which may be a horizon marker for this period. Stoltman (personal communication) estimates that between 20 to 30 have been found on Minnesota Laurel sites. These artifacts are most likely related to sturgeon fishing, and this is supported in the archaeological record where sturgeon are the most frequent faunal remains. Wright (1967:39) recovered three harpoon heads from the Heron Bay site on the Pic River, however none are reported from Anderson or Nutimik focus sites and none were found at Naomikong Point.

North of the Rainy River area a partial list of sites includes, the Swan Lake (Kenyon, 1961) and the Pelican Falls (Wright, 1967) sites, while to the east a series of sites have been located inland and along the north shore of Lake Superior as far east as Agawa Bay. Among these sites are; Pays Platt, Killala Lake, Little Pic, Heron Bay, Michipicoten Harbor, and Sand River (Wright, 1967). In both the northern and southern areas Laurel sites take on a different appearance from the Rainy River sites, in so far as the diagnostic burial mound is absent. Pottery continues to be composed of the same basic set of attributes, although certain ones, such as bossing, decrease in frequency. The lithic assemblage is still dominated by scrapers which at the Heron Bay site outnumber the total of all other flint artifacts four to one. This latter site is the largest of the Northern Ontario Laurel sites and the inventory is impressive with the larger artifact categories represented by; 2,749 sherds, 598 scrapers, 46 projectile points, and 118 copper artifacts. For most of the other sites strung along the north shore of Lake Superior very little material has been recovered. The second largest site is Killala Lake with a total archaeological assemblage of 167 items, and next is Pays Platt with only 119 artifacts. Another small site is the Sand River site located on the northeastern shore of Lake Superior on Agawa Bay. This site is important for two reasons; first because it is one of the few sites with a radiocarbon date, and second because of its proximity to the Naomikong Point site. On the first count, a radiocarbon date of A.D. 320 ± 100 (M-1507) (Crane and Griffin, 1965:130-31) was obtained on material taken from a hearth deposit. Second, the Sand River site is almost directly north of the Naomikong Point site, and by land the two sites are approximately 70 miles apart, however a direct water route reduces the distance to about 40 miles. (Thus these two sites established a continuity of Laurel sites between the north and south shore of Lake Superior.)

The identification of Laurel material at Naomikong Point naturally aroused interest in this area, and in July, 1967, Jeffrey Briggs and Charles Taylor conducted a survey for the University of Michigan Museum of Anthropology. They thoroughly investigated an area from Grand Marais, Michigan to Marquette, Michigan along the south shore of Lake Superior without discovering a single site or prehistoric artifact or flint chip.

The Naomikong Point Model

In the preceding section a thumbnail sketch of the areal distribution of Laurel sites has been presented.

There are certain problems that arise in attempting to compare the Naomikong Point data with those from other Laurel sites. First of all, the nature of the sites must be considered. The model being tested is derived from data obtained from a village site. Such a model would be difficult to test with data derived from a burial mound. A second factor which must be considered is the variation in size of Laurel sites. Many are very small and the quantity of material which has been recovered seems to indicate a short-term occupation. It can even be questioned if any site is of sufficient magnitude to test this model. A check of the literature reveals that the total ceramic assemblage from Laurel components in Minnesota, Manitoba, and Northern Ontario is in the range of 22,000 sherds. At Naomikong Point, Laurel sherds with a dimension of one inch and greater, numbered around 17,000. This may indicate that Naomikong Point was occupied longer and/or more intensely than other known Laurel sites.

A more serious problem which is faced in testing the Naomikong Point model relates to the way Laurel sites have been excavated and the manner in which the data has been handled. The subject here is not "good" or "bad" field techniques and data handling, but instead to point out once again, that different techniques are used by archaeologists attempting to solve different kinds of problems. To date, the main efforts have been directed towards defining the temporal and spatial limits of Laurel. This is a vital step that must preface any attempt to probe the cultural dimension. An excavation unit of 10 by 10 feet can be used effectively to investigate temporal-spatial problems, however, a smaller-sized unit is more desirable for developing the cultural picture. Greater confidence can be placed statistically in a correlation coefficient computed in terms of 16, 5- by 5-foot units than one obtained from 4, 10- by 10-foot units.

With these problems in mind, Laurel sites will be examined in terms of the cultural picture derived from Naomikong Point. Certain constants seem to underlie all Laurel sites, and primary among these is site location. All sites are adjacent to either lakes or rivers. This would seem to suggest that these were favorable locations for fishing, however, the low pH soil at most sites is sufficiently acid to destroy bone, and thus the implied reliance on fishing cannot be verified. At those sites where there is bone preservation, such as the Heron Bay site (Wright, 1967:41 and the Manitoba sites (MacNeish, 1958) a mixed hunting and fishing subsistence pattern can be inferred from the faunal remains. The developmental sequence derived by MacNeish (1958) for Manitoba shows continuity from the Archaic Whiteshell focus (3000 to 1500 B.C.) to the Selkirk focus (A.D. 1350 to 1750). The subsistence pattern throughout this sequence is one of greater and greater dependence on fishing. The Anderson focus is seen as a relatively balanced hunting and fishing economy while fish is considered more widely utilized than mammal in the Nutimik focus. It may be erroneous to consider Middle Woodland fishing villages in the same light as the Chippewa village at Sault Ste. Marie which Schoolcraft described (Williams, 1953:95-96):

> There are at present, about forty lodges of Chippeway Indians, containing a population of about two hundred souls, who subsist wholly upon the white-fish.

Another characteristic of Laurel sites is the high frequency of side and end scrapers. This is particularly true for Northern Ontario Laurel sites and the Naomikong Point site. Fitting (1967: 241), has contrasted the faunal remains and flint tools from several sites, and has hypothesized that unifacial tools will be more frequent than bifacial tools at fishing stations, while the reverse will be found at hunting sites. At those Anderson and Nutimik focus sites which have faunal data, fish comprises 47 percent of the faunal remains in Anderson focus sites, and the uniface to biface ratio is approximately one to one, while a three to one ratio occurs for the Nutimik focus where fish represent 87 percent of the faunal remains. These ratios are based on projectile points and bifacial blades (preforms) in the biface category and scrapers in the uniface category. There is no information on unifacially-worked flakes, and therefore these data could not be included in the proportions. The uniface to biface ratio (excluding unifacially worked flakes) at other Laurel sites is: Pays Platt (20:1), Heron Bay (7:1), Killala Lake (3:1), Rossport (2:1), and Little Pic (1:1). At the Naomikong Point site this ratio is a staggering 35:1. If Fitting's hypothesis can be demonstrated to have a relatively high degree of validity, then the interpretation of the Naomikong Point site as a fishing village would gain support.

A third characteristic shared by Laurel sites is a ceramic assemblage which derives its decorative elements from a common attribute pool. This statement is actually a truism since pottery is the basic defining criterion for Laurel. Vessels are conoidal-based and decoration is confined to the upper one-half to one-third of the vessel. The undecorated portion is smoothed and cord-marking is absent. A description and discussion of Laurel pottery has already been presented. Other than to emphasize the participation in an intraregional ceramic complex no additional remarks will be made.

At most Laurel sites chipping debris from artifact manufacturing is present. The high frequency of decortication flakes, block flakes, and cores associated with finished artifacts indicates that raw material was being converted into finished artifacts at these sites. In almost all cases the material could be obtained locally, however, as at Naomikong Point, obsidian is sometimes found on Laurel sites. Wright (1967:32) reports an obsidian scraper and flake from the Heron Bay site, and cites a personal communication from W. A. Kenyon as to the presence of obsidian in Laurel sites along the Ontario side of the Rainy River. Wilford (1952) has also reported obsidian samples from the Pike Bay Mound in Minnesota.

One inconsistent feature of the Laurel culture is the variability in the size of sites. Some sites cover a considerable area and produce an artifact assemblage that numbers in the thousands while other sites yield only a few sherds, one or two scrapers, and some chippage debris. If site size can be correlated with group size, then the smaller sites may represent single family units while the larger ones correspond to larger groups which may be unrelated. Such a situation is suggestive of a seasonally-based economy where the population is dispersed during part of the year, operating in small one or two family units. During other parts of the year these groups coalesce into villages for the purpose of exploiting a locally abundant food resource. Fishing is seen as a subsistence base that could generate a cohesive force of this kind. During the spawning season a reliable and abundant source of food would be available and a stable village life could be supported. It is doubtful if at any time of the year mammal hunting could match the potential food resource of fish and thus act as a catalyst for the formation of large village sites.

A summary of some of the more prominent characteristics of Laurel sites has been presented. The motivation has been to establish a background against which the model derived for

Naomikong Point could be tested. In general, many sites display the proper credential in terms of artifactual and non-artifactual assemblages to indicate a similar way of life to the groups at Naomikong Point. Only one site, the Heron Bay site, (Wright, 1967:5-41), seems to have some of the necessary ingredients that are required to make a partial test of the Naomikong Point model. This site has the largest Laurel component of any Northern Ontario site and in the approximately 1,500 square feet that were excavated a wide range of archaeological data were recovered. A sample of carbon scraped from the interior of sherds yielded a radiocarbon date of A.D. 140 ± 150 years (G.S.C.-686). Of particular interest at the site is the post mold and feature distribution. Twenty-five post molds and two features were concentrated in an area of about 20 feet by 10 feet. Two other features occurred about 15 and 30 feet away. The post mold pattern is erratic and does not seem to define the outline of a structure. All four features were interpreted as hearths and contained mostly fire-cracked rock and chipping debris. The association of post molds with features follows the pattern observed at Naomikong Point.

In describing the cultural deposit Wright states (1967:7):

> The cultural deposit tended to be relatively uniform with regard to artifact production, and the materials from widely separated excavation units were generally similar in both quantity and variety.

The same words could be applied to the Naomikong Point site as it was being excavated. It was only when the product-moment correlation test was run that a differential relationship among artifact classes was recognized. It is tempting to suggest that the same kinds of activities, subsistence and settlement patterns, and types of social organization are present at Heron Bay as at Naomikong Point.

It is unfortunate that the Naomikong Point model cannot be tested against more sites, but at the present time pertinent types of both data and sites are absent. The model will now be viewed in terms of Laurel's neighboring cultures.

NORTHERN LAKE MICHIGAN

Some indications of Laurel have been found in the northern Lake Michigan area, although at the present time there are no known sites bridging this region with the Superior Basin. In northwestern Lake Michigan Mason has defined the North Bay

Culture from two sites on the Door Peninsula of Wisconsin (Mason, 1966 and 1967). This culture, as known from the Mero and Porte des Morts sites, shows an involvement with both the Hopewellian Havana tradition from the south, and Laurel cultures to the north. The ceramic types; North Bay Dentate, North Bay Scallop, and North Bay Linear Stamped all show a strong similarity to Laurel types. The non-ceramic inventory also displays Laurel traits and the toggle head harpoon is an artifact type shared with Minnesota Laurel. The almost equal proportion of projectile points and scrapers deviates from the Laurel pattern, particularly in Northern Ontario and at the Naomikong Point site. A radiocarbon date of A.D. 160 ± 100 (I-888) from the Porte des Morts site falls nicely into place with the Heron Bay date of A.D. 140 ± 150 (G.S.C.-686).

On Summer Island, which is located in northern Lake Michigan between the Garden Peninsula of Michigan and the Door Peninsula of Wisconsin, David Brose has excavated a stratified site with a Middle Woodland component. The Middle Woodland component has been interpreted as a mid-spring to early fall sturgeon fishing village and has been radiocarbon dated at A.D. 250 ± 150 (M-1985) (Brose, personal communication). Many of the diagnostic Laurel features are missing at this site. Ceramics are more frequently decorated with a simple tool than a dentate tool and not one example of pseudo-scallop shell decoration is present in the 7,000 sherd assemblage. The presence of only 50 or 60 scrapers does not reflect the involvement with this implement suggested by other Laurel sites.

In August 1965, Earl Prahl surveyed the north shore of Lake Michigan in the vicinity of Seul Choix Point where Laurel-like ceramics were recovered from the Ekdahl-Goodreau site (Prahl, personal communication). The decoration on some of the sherds corresponds to what has been called the Naomikong Point variety of Laurel Pseudo-scallop Shell. Both dentate and simple tool decoration shows application by a drag-stamping technique.

Although not in the Northern Lake Michigan area, two sites which seem to be culturally involved with this region are the Arrowhead Drive and Goodwin-Gresham sites. The former is located on Bois Blanc Island in the Straits of Mackinac and consists of an ossuary of eight burials. A radiocarbon date of A.D. 50 ± 120 (M-1392) (Crane and Griffin, 1965:129) was obtained on the skeletal material thus placing the ossuary in the Middle Woodland period. Associated burial goods included portions of a conoidal-based vessel decorated with large cross-hatched incisions. Other pottery found in the ossuary included sherds decorated with either a simple or dentate tool applied in a drag-stamped fashion (Bettarel and Harrison, 1962:37-42).

The Goodwin-Gresham site was excavated by the University Museum of Anthropology in the summer of 1964. The site is located in northeastern Michigan near the mouth of the Au Sable River and is the southernmost site in Michigan which can be considered part of the Northern Middle Woodland pattern. The ceramics from the site are anomalous, showing affinities with cultures to the east and west. Some sherds could probably be classified as Becker Punctate (Brose, personal communication), indicating ties with the North Bay Culture, while dentate and rocker-stamped sherds and a high frequency of interior channeling show affiliations with cultures to the east. Fitting (1965) states: "This site produced cultural material of a type which could broadly be referred to as Point Peninsula II."

THE SAUGEEN FOCUS

In the discussion of the spatial distribution of Laurel sites a blending of Laurel with the North Bay culture of Wisconsin was noted. An interaction of Laurel is also seen in Southern Ontario. In this area James V. Wright (Wright and Anderson, 1963), has defined the Saugeen focus. This focus is the product of components from the Donaldson, Inverheron, Burley, Newman, and Short sites. Temporally, the Saugeen focus has been dated by two radiocarbon dates. A date of 530 B.C. ± 60 years (S-119) (McCallum and Wittenberg, 1962:77) was obtained for the Donaldson site and 669 B.C. ± 200 years (C-192) for the basal component at the Burley site. These dates are 500 years earlier than any date obtained for Laurel, and if Farrand's (1962:187-89) determination for the separation of Lakes Superior and Huron is correct, Naomikong Point was still underwater. Indeed Naomikong Point is a cultural backwash. Mason (1967:337) has questioned the validity of these dates pointing out that they are inconsistent with all Middle Woodland dates. Culturally Laurel and Saugeen appear to be contemporary Middle Woodland groups sharing common cultural elements.

In terms of artifact assemblages, the similarities between Laurel and Saugeen are reflected in the pottery. Both cultures share the pseudo-scallop shell motif and at the Donaldson site this was the most frequently occurring decoration. It is interesting to note that the two most frequent styles of pseudo-scallop shell decoration at the Donaldson site are; one or more rows of obliques, or one row of obliques over horizontals. These same two styles seem to have been culturally preferred at the Naomikong Point site. At the Inverhuron site pseudo-scallop shell decoration is scarce and calls to mind similar intrasite ceramic differences in the Laurel culture.

Dentate-stamped pottery occurs much more frequently on Saugeen sites than on Laurel sites, and the presence of rocker stamping on the former serves as an important attribute for distinguishing the two cultures. Rocker stamping is a distinctive trait of Hopewell, and thus Saugeen ceramics appear to be an amalgamation of Laurel, Hopewell, and, as will be discussed later, Point Peninsula.

Since the Donaldson site is the largest of the Saugeen sites it will serve as the focal point for the remainder of this discussion. Material from the lithic assemblage appears to have been largely locally derived, and the presence of 17 pounds of chippage debris is an indication that all stages of flint tool manufacturing were performed at the site. Bifacially worked tools consist of 17 projectile points and 8 blades, while 79 scrapers comprise the unifacial tools. A uniface to biface ratio of approximately three to one corresponds exactly with the ratio obtained from the Nutimik focus data. Certain items in the stone tool inventory from the Donaldson site are not typically Laurel, and these are, anvil stones, pestles, a mortar, and gorgets.

Non-artifactual data include approximately 300 post molds from which Wright (Wright and Anderson, 1963:11-15) delineated two houses. Associated with these houses are features which appear to be hearths and pits whose function is unknown. Northwest of the houses is a small cemetery which consisted of 6 graves containing 12 individuals. Faunal remains from the site are dominated by fish, of which sturgeon is the most prevalent. In contrast to the Naomikong Point site only one net sinker was recovered from the Donaldson site. If there is any validity in the inferred function of the net sinker it may be that sturgeon were not taken in nets; this technique was perhaps used for smaller fish. Very few bone tools were found at the Donaldson site and no toggle head harpoons were recovered.

The general impression of the Donaldson site is that the people were living in much the same way as the people at Naomikong Point. Both were exploiting local stone resources and manufacturing flint tools at the site. The small, social units postulated for Naomikong Point is reflected at the Donaldson site in small, "family-sized" houses. Both sites were fishing villages (inferred for the Naomikong Point site), however, one group is concentrating on sturgeon while the other is presumably taking whitefish.

It is interesting to speculate whether different fishing patterns are associated with different types of social organization and group structure. The model derived for Naomikong Point may breakdown in terms of the postulated independent family unit, and greater group cooperation and participation may be associated with sturgeon fishing. A model derived for the Saugeen focus might provide interesting results.

POINT PENINSULA

The Point Peninsula II culture of the Middle Woodland period displays a number of cultural similarities to both Laurel and Saugeen. Spatially the culture is centered in Southern Ontario, portions of New York State, and Southern Quebec. Geographical continuity with the Laurel culture is represented by several sites among which are the Sheguiandah, Killarney, and Frank Bay sites. The Sheguiandah site on Manitoulin Island and the Killarney site at the north end of Georgian Bay both yielded a small assemblage of pseudo-scallop shell sherds. At the latter site the Middle Woodland materials have been radiocarbon dated at 80 ± 200 B.C. (M-428) (Crane and Griffin, 1959). The Frank Bay site at the southern end of Lake Nipissing (Ridley, 1954), shows a blending of Laurel and Point Peninsula ceramic characteristics. Decorative elements include pseudo-scallop shell and dentate and rocker stamping. One sherd displays an interesting combination with the interior decorated by rockered dentate stamping, while the exterior has a rim decorated with pseudo-scallop shell impressions below which is dentate stamping.

To the east, the Point Peninsula culture extends up the St. Lawrence River and filters eastward to the Atlantic Coast. Since the Point Peninsula culture encompasses a large geographical area and is represented by many sites, a thorough survey of the culture would involve a lengthy discussion. The main purpose of introducing Point Peninsula is to demonstrate that during Middle Woodland times Laurel participated in a cultural medium which extends far beyond the Lake Superior Basin.

The major cultural similarity underlying Laurel, Saugeen, and Point Peninsula is pottery. In fact what is referred to as a cultural tradition may be in reality a ceramic tradition. Ritchie (1965:204) states:

The appearance . . . of pseudo-scallop shell, dentate, complex dentate, and rocker-stamped styles is taken as the marker for the inception of the Point Peninsula culture of the Middle Woodland period in the Northeast.

The presence of pseudo-scallop shell decorated pottery indicates ties with Laurel to the southwest while rocker-stamped pottery is a characteristic of Hopewell to the southeast. On Southern Ontario Point Peninsula sites pseudo-scallop shell decoration is more frequent than rocker stamping, while the reverse is found on New York sites.

Besides ceramic similarities the presence of burial mounds indicates strong Hopewellian influence in Point Peninsula. The main concentration of mounds is in the Rice Lake area of Southern Ontario and western New York State. In the former area, excavations of the Serpent Mounds site (Johnston, 1968) and the Cameron's Point site (Spence and Harper, 1968) show a grafting of Hopewellian and Point Peninsula cultural elements. A greater number of mounds have been located in western New York, and the intensity of Hopewellian influence in this area appears to have been greater than in Southern Ontario. Ritchie (1965:214) has classified the New York burial mounds as the Squawkie Hill phase of the Hopewellian cultural manifestation in the Northeast.

The presence of burial mounds in Minnesota Laurel and Point Peninsula indicates an interaction between northern and southern Middle Woodland cultures. The Havana and Laurel elements seen in the North Bay culture point suspiciously toward Illinois Hopewell as the culture influencing Laurel. Point Peninsula, on the other hand, probably derived elements of Hopewellian culture from Ohio. Although Northern Middle Woodland groups engaged in a cultural symbiosis with peoples to the south, they should not be thought of as "half-baked" Hopewellians. Laurel, North Bay, Saugeen, and Point Peninsula are also interacting, and the basic cultural elements of these groups are probably strongly directed toward exploitation of, and adaptation to, a Lake Forest ecological zone.

SUMMARY

In this section a brief summary of Northern Middle Woodland cultures has been presented. Laurel has received the most attention, and in particular the cultural dimension has been accented. From an archaeological point of view Laurel has developed from a focus on the Rainy River to a culture occupying the greater part of the Lake Superior Basin. It was found that the cultural model of Laurel derived from the excavations at Naomikong Point could only partially be tested because of a lack of comparable data from other sites. Artifact inventories and their relative proportions from the larger Laurel sites were found to be compatible, and the post mold and feature pattern at the Heron Bay site was very similar to that found at the Naomikong Point site. A social structure based on the family operating as an independent unit could not be verified. A subsistence pattern oriented toward fishing is inferred from site location, although hunting was also important as seen in Anderson focus sites.

Temporally Laurel can be placed somewhere around the time of Christ to about A.D. 450; the Naomikong Point date defining the upper limits of the culture. The origin of the Laurel culture has not been discussed, however, two conflicting theories are present. The majority of archaeologists would derive Laurel out of local Archaic cultures which, through time, are able to exploit the environment more and more efficiently. James V. Wright (1967:130-35) has recently opposed this position pointing out the lack of artifact continuity between Archaic and Woodland cultures. His Hypothesis 2 states that "The Laurel Tradition is of Asiatic origin." This is based solely on the similarities of ceramic motif shared by Laurel and eastern Asiatic cultures. The Naomikong Point excavations did not provide any additional data to either support or reject this hypothesis.

The other Northern Middle Woodland cultures, North Bay, Saugeen, and Point Peninsula all seem to be interacting with Laurel as well as with each other. Laurel and North Bay features are seen at the Porte des Morts site while North Bay and Point Peninsula appear to be fused at the Goodwin-Gresham site. The Donaldson site shows Saugeen occurring with some Laurel and Point Peninsula characteristics, while Laurel and Point Peninsula cultural elements occur at the Sheguiandah, Killarney, and Frank Bay sites. All these cultures appear to be participating in an intraregional ceramic complex, and pottery is the basic common denominator which ties together the Northern Middle Woodland cultures.

Even though the archaeologist has speciated these cultures it may prove advantageous to think in terms of one large cultural unit rather than several smaller ones. The unifying feature of Northern Middle Woodland groups may be the particular ecological conditions of the Lake Forest area. The adaptation and exploitation of this ecological zone by prehistoric populations may show a greater cultural consistency than demonstrated by their pottery. The Naomikong Point site was excavated and analyzed in terms of probing the cultural dimension and extracting information regarding the interaction of prehistoric groups and their environment. Unfortunately the model derived from the Naomikong Point site for the Laurel culture stands alone. There is very little of the right kinds of data from other archaeological sites to test this model. While the temporal and spatial dimensions of Northern Middle Woodland should not be neglected, an invitation is extended to archaeologists working in this area to derive cultural models from their data. Hopefully more reliable models than the one derived from Naomikong Point will be conceived, and from these a more accurate picture of the cultural dimension will unfold.

APPENDIX I

CHI-SQUARE TABLES FOR CERAMIC ATTRIBUTE ASSOCIATIONS*

*When a second chi-square value in parentheses is given after the first, it is the figure obtained when correction for continuity has been applied.

LAUREL PSEUDO-SCALLOP SHELL

Attributes	First Absent/ Second Absent		First Absent/ Second Present		First Present/ Second Absent		First Present/ Second Present		Chi-Square	
	Observed	Expected	Observed	Expected	Observed	Expected	Observed	Expected		
Straight rim/Punctuations	32	27.8	5	9.2	38	42.2	18	13.8	4.15	
Vertical rim decoration/ Bossing	70	67.0	5	8.0	13	16.0	5	2.0	6.74	(4.40)
Horizontal body decoration/ Rim and body decorated alike	9	28.6	39	19.4	42	22.4	3	22.6	52.17	
Horizontal body decoration/ Punctuations	29	36.1	19	11.9	41	33.9	4	11.1	11.76	
Oblique body decoration/ Vertical rim decoration	39	46.0	18	11.0	36	29.0	0	7.0	14.10	
Oblique body decoration/ Oblique rim decoration	31	37.4	26	19.6	30	23.6	6	12.4	8.19	
Oblique body decoration/ Bossing	47	50.9	10	6.1	36	32.1	0	3.9	7.08	(5.43)
Horizontal body decoration/ Vertical rim decoration	47	38.7	1	9.3	28	36.3	17	8.7	18.96	
Horizontal body decoration/ Oblique rim decoration	41	31.5	7	16.5	20	29.5	25	15.5	17.28	
Horizontal body decoration/ Bossing	47	42.8	1	5.2	36	40.2	9	4.8	7.77	(6.13)
Oblique body decoration/ Rim and body decorated alike	44	31.3	13	25.7	7	19.7	29	16.3	29.71	
Oblique body/Punctuations	51	42.9	6	14.1	19	27.1	17	8.9	15.96	
Rim and body decorated alike/ Punctuations	43	38.3	8	12.7	27	31.7	15	10.3	4.96	
Rim and body decorated alike/ Bossing	42	45.5	9	5.5	41	37.5	1	4.5	5.59	(4.26)

LAUREL PSEUDO-SCALLOP SHELL NAOMIKONG POINT VARIETY

Attributes	First Absent/ Second Absent		First Absent/ Second Present		First Present/ Second Absent		First Present/ Second Present		Chi-Square
	Observed	Expected	Observed	Expected	Observed	Expected	Observed	Expected	
Straight rim/Interior decoration	23	17.9	4	9.1	18	23.1	17	11.9	7.75
Straight rim/Drag stamp	21	17.0	6	10.0	18	22.0	17	13.0	4.53
Interior decoration/Lip decoration	33	27.1	8	13.9	8	13.9	13	7.1	11.14
Interior decoration/Punctations	33	27.8	8	13.2	9	14.2	12	6.8	9.00
Outsloping rim/Interior decoration	20	24.4	17	12.6	21	16.6	4	8.4	5.97
Outsloping rim/Drag stamp	19	23.3	18	13.7	20	15.7	5	9.3	5.25
Vertical body decoration/ Lip decoration	29	33.0	21	17.0	12	8.0	0	4.0	7.62 (5.70)
Straight rim/Punctations	40	35.6	4	8.4	32	36.4	13	8.6	5.64
Oblique body decoration/ Rim and body decorated alike	13	5.8	6	13.2	14	12.2	56	48.8	16.58
Oblique body decoration/ Drag stamp	17	11.5	2	7.5	37	42.5	33	27.5	8.40
Plain body/Oblique rim decoration	74	66.6	3	10.4	3	10.4	9	1.6	45.00 (39.60)
Outsloping rim/Punctations	39	42.9	14	10.1	33	29.1	3	6.9	4.54
Oblique body decoration/ Oblique rim decoration	8	16.4	11	2.6	69	60.6	1	9.4	40.85 (35.46)

APPENDIX II

CORRELATION COEFFICIENTS OVER .80

Total Site	
Coefficient	Test
.80	Total no. chippage/scrapers
.83	Total no. chippage/decortication flakes
.88	Total no. chippage/block flakes
.93	Total no. chippage/flat flakes
East of discontinuity	
.80	Total no. chippage/scrapers
.80	Total no. chippage/decortication flakes
.93	Total no. chippage/flat flakes
.95	Total no. chippage/block flakes
.90	Flat flakes/block flakes
.82	Work flakes/scrapers
West of discontinuity	
.88	Scrapers/total sherds
.83	Scrapers/total no. chippage
.83	Scrapers/decortication flakes
.85	Scrapers/block flakes
.93	Scrapers/flat flakes
.83	Total sherds/total no. chippage
.83	Flakes of bifacial retouch/hard hammer flakes
.82	Flakes of bifacial retouch/worked flakes
.82	Total pieces of copper/decortication flakes
.83	Heat-treated flakes/block flakes
.84	Heat-treated flakes/total no. chippage
.80	Block flakes/bipolar cores
Unit A	
Coefficient	Test
.90	Total no. chippage/block flakes
.97	Total no. chippage/flat flakes
.82	Block flakes/flat flakes
.95	Total no. worked flakes/scrapers
.80	Soft hammer flakes/hard hammer flakes
.84	Weight of fire-cracked rock/total no. cores
Unit C	
.91	Total no. chippage/block flakes
.83	Total no. chippage/flat flakes
.85	Block flakes/flat flakes
.81	Flakes of bifacial retouch/hard hammer flakes

APPENDIX II (Cont'd.)

Unit D	
.87	Total no. sherds/scrapers
.87	Total no. chippage/decortication flakes
.84	Total pieces of copper/decortication flakes
.82	Total weight calcined bone/block flakes
Unit E	
.83	Total no. chippage/block flakes
.90	Total no. chippage/flat flakes
.87	Total no. chippage/decortication flakes
.83	Quartz flakes/decortication flakes
.82	Quartz flakes/total no. chippage
.80	Quartz artifacts/hard hammer flakes
.87	Flakes of bifacial retouch/hard hammer flakes
.90	Total no. sherds/preforms
.83	Total weight calcined bone/preforms
.80	Total no. cores/Laurel Pseudo-scallop Shell Naomikong Point Variety

REFERENCES

Baerreis, David A. and Reid A. Bryson
1965 Climatic Episodes and the Dating of Mississippian Cultures. The Wisconsin Archaeologist, Vol. 46, No. 4:203-20. Lake Mills.

Bettarel, Robert and Sidney Harrison
1962 An Early Ossuary in Michigan. Michigan Archaeologist, Vol. 8, No. 4:37-42. Ann Arbor.

Binford, Lewis R. and George I. Quimby
1963 Indian Sites and Chipped Stone Material in the Northern Lake Michigan Area. Fieldiana: Anthropology, Vol. 36:227-307. Chicago.

Blalock, Hubert M.
1960 Social Statistics. McGraw-Hill Book Co., Inc. New York.

Brown, James A.
1962 Notes and News. American Antiquity, Vol. 28, No. 1:120. Salt Lake City.

Buckman, Harry O. and Nyle C. Brady
1965 The Nature and Properties of Soils. The Macmillan Co. New York.

Burt, William H. and Richard P. Grossenheider
1964 A Field Guide to the Mammals. Houghton Mifflin Co. Boston.

Cleland, Charles Edward
1966 The Prehistoric Animal Ecology and Ethnozoology of the Upper Great Lakes Region. Anthropological Papers No. 29, Museum of Anthropology, University of Michigan. Ann Arbor.

Crane, H. R. and J. B. Griffin
1959 University of Michigan Radiocarbon Dates IV. American Journal of Science Radiocarbon Supplement, Vol. 1:183. New Haven.
1960 University of Michigan Radiocarbon Dates V. American Journal of Science Radiocarbon Supplement, Vol. 2:31-48. New Haven.
1965 University of Michigan Radiocarbon Dates X. American Journal of Science Radiocarbon Supplement, Vol. 7:129-31. New Haven.

Cushing, Edward J.
1965 Problems in the Quaternary Phytogeography of the Great Lakes Region. *In*: The Quaternary of the United States, edited by H. E. Wright, Jr. and David G. Frey, Princeton University Press. Princeton.

Dice, Lee R.
1943 The Biotic Provinces of North America. University of Michigan Press. Ann Arbor.

Edminster, Frank C.
1947 The Ruffed Grouse. Macmillan Co. New York.

Eichmeier, A. H.
1964 Climate of Michigan. *In*: Readings in the Geography of Michigan. Edited by Charles M. Davis. Ann Arbor Publishers. Ann Arbor.

Farrand, William R.
1962 Postglacial Uplift in North America. American Journal of Science. Vol. 260:181-99.

Fitting, James E.
1965 Middle Woodland Manifestations in Eastern Michigan. Paper presented at the 30th Annual Meeting of the Society for American Archaeology. Urbana.
1967 The Camp of the Careful Indian: An Upper Great Lakes Chipping Station. Papers of the Michigan Academy of Science, Arts, and Letters. Vol. LII:237-42. Ann Arbor.
n.d. The Archaeological Potential of Naomikong Point. Manuscript on file at University of Michigan Museum of Anthropology.

Fitting, James E., Jerry DeVisscher, and Edward J. Wahala
1966 The Paleo-Indian Occupation of the Holcombe Beach. Anthropological Papers No. 27, Museum of Anthropology University of Michigan. Ann Arbor.

Griffin, James B., *et al.*
n.d. Identification of the Sources of Hopewellian Obsidian in the Middle West (manuscript submitted to American Antiquity).

Hill, E. B. and Russell G. Mawby
1964 Types of Farming in Michigan. *In:* Readings in the Geography of Michigan. Edited by Charles M. Davis, Ann Arbor Publishers. Ann Arbor.

Hinsdale, W. B.
1931 Archaeological Atlas of Michigan. Michigan Handbook Series, No. 4. University of Michigan Press. Ann Arbor.

Hough, Jack L.
1958 Geology of the Great Lakes. University of Illinois Press. Urbana.
1963 The Prehistoric Great Lakes of North America. American Scientist, Vol. 51, No. 1:84-109. Easton.

Hubbs, Carl L. and Karl F. Lagler
1958 Fishes of the Great Lakes Region. University of Michigan Press. Ann Arbor.

Johnston, Richard B.
1968 The Archaeology of the Serpent Mounds Site. Occasional Paper 10, Art and Archaeology Division, The Royal Ontario Museum. Toronto.

Kenyon, W. A.
1960 Rainy River Project—1959. Ontario History, Vol. LII, No. 1. Toronto.
1961 The Swan Lake Site. Occasional Paper 1. Royal Ontario Museum, Art and Archaeology Division. Toronto.

McCallum, K. J. and J. Wittenberg
1962 University of Saskatchewan Radiocarbon Dates III. American Journal of Science Radiocarbon Supplement, Vol. 4:77.

McPerron, Alan
1967 The Juntunen Site and the Late Woodland Prehistory of the Upper Great Lakes Area. Anthropological Paper No. 30, Museum of Anthropology, University of Michigan. Ann Arbor.

MacNeish, Richard S.
1954 The Scott Mound and Village, Near Brandon, Manitoba. Annual Report of the National Museum of Canada 1952-53:20-65. Ottawa.
1958 An Introduction to the Archaeology of Southeast Manitoba. National Museum of Canada, Bulletin 157. Ottawa.

Mason, Philip
1958 Schoolcraft's Expedition to Lake Itasca. Michigan State University Press. East Lansing.

Mason, Ronald J.
1966 Two Stratified Sites on the Door Peninsula of Wisconsin. Anthropological Paper No. 26, Museum of Anthropology University of Michigan. Ann Arbor.
1967 The North Bay Component at the Porte des Morts Site, Door County, Wisconsin. The Wisconsin Archaeologist, Vol. 48, No. 4:267-345. Lake Mills.

Pitezel, John H.
1901 The Life of Peter Marksman. Western Methodist Book Concern. Cincinnati.

Potzger, J. E.
1946 Phytosociology of the Primeval Forest in Central-Northern Wisconsin and Upper Michigan and a Brief Post—Glacial History of the Lake Forest Formation. Ecological Monographs, Vol. 16:211-50. Duke University Press. Durham.

Quimby, George I.
1965 Exploring an Underwater Indian Site. Chicago Natural History Museum Bulletin, Vol. 36, No. 8:2-4. Chicago.

Ridley, Frank
1954 The Frank Bay Site, Lake Nipissing, Ontario. American Antiquity, Vol. 20, No. 1:40-50. Salt Lake City.

Ritchie, William A.
1965 The Archaeology of New York State. The Natural History Press. New York.

Rouse, Irving
1960 The Classification of Artifacts in Archaeology. American Antiquity, Vol. 25, No. 3:313-25.

Shelford, Victor E.
1963 The Ecology of North America. University of Illinois Press. Urbana.

Spence, Michael W. and J. Russell Harper
1968 The Cameron's Point Site. Occasional Paper 12, Art and Archaeology Division, Royal Ontario Museum. Toronto.

Stoltman, James B.
1962 A Proposed Method of Systematizing the Modal of Analysis of Pottery and Its Application to the Laurel Focus. M.A. Thesis, University of Minnesota. Minneapolis.

Whiteside, E. P., J. F. Schneider, and R. L. Cook
1964 The Soils of Michigan. *In:* Readings in the Geography of Michigan. Edited by Charles M. Davis. Ann Arbor Publishers. Ann Arbor.

Wilford, Lloyd A.
1952 The Prehistoric Indians of Minnesota. Minnesota Archaeologist, Vol. 18, No. 2. Minneapolis.

Williams, Mentor L.
1953 Narrative Journal of Travels Through the Northwestern Regions of the United States Extending from Detroit Through the Great Chain of American Lakes to the Sources of the Mississippi River in the Year 1820, by Henry R. Schoolcraft. Michigan State College Press. East Lansing.

Witthoff, John
1957 The Art of Flint Chipping. Ohio Archeologist, Vol. 7:17-20ff. Columbus.

Wright, J. V.
1963 An Archaeological Survey Along the North Shore of Lake Superior. Anthropology Papers, National Museum of Canada, No. 3. Ottawa.
1967 The Laurel Tradition and the Middle Woodland Period. National Museum of Canada, Bulletin 217. Ottawa.

Wright, James V. and J. E. Anderson
1963 The Donaldson Site. National Museum of Canada, Bulletin 184. Ottawa.

The Naomikong Point site:
a) Menekaunee Point as seen from the site.

b) Excavating Unit D.

North Wall Profile of 5- by 60-foot trench: *a*) Eastern end of trench; *b*) Western end of trench.

Laurel Pseudo-scallop Shell vessel fragment from the Naomikong Point site.

PLATE IV

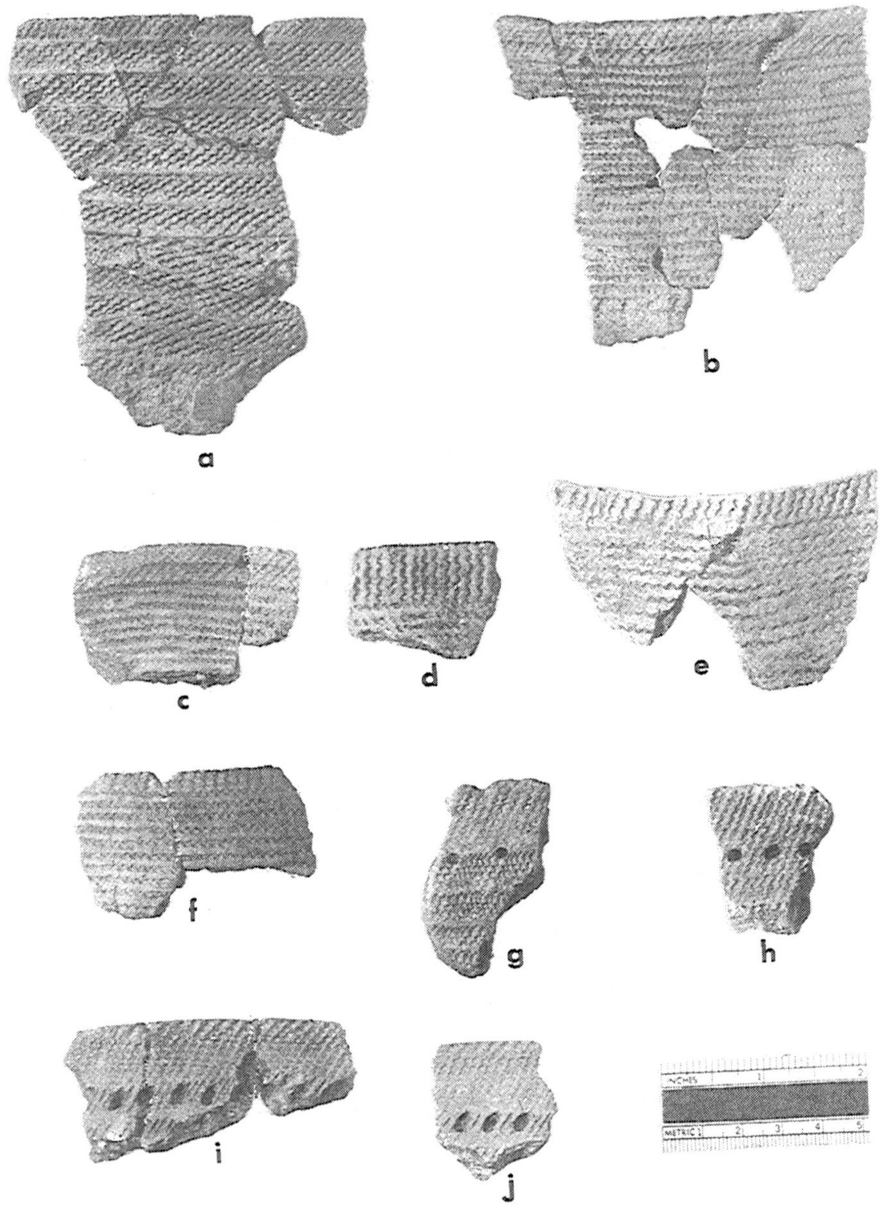

Laurel Pseudo-scallop Shell rim sherds from the Naomikong Point site.

Laurel Pseudo-scallop Shell Naomikong Point Variety vessel fragment.

PLATE VI

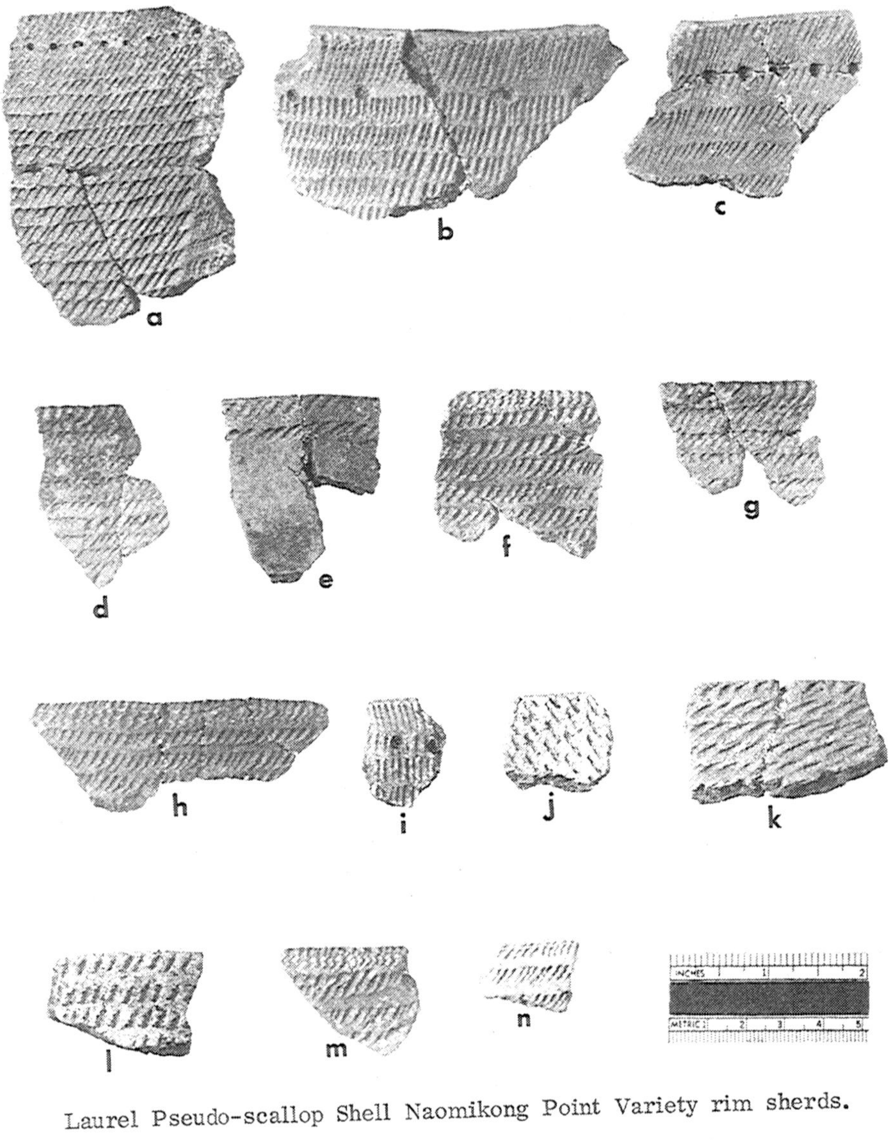

Laurel Pseudo-scallop Shell Naomikong Point Variety rim sherds.

Sherds from the Naomikong Point site showing combined decoration techniques.

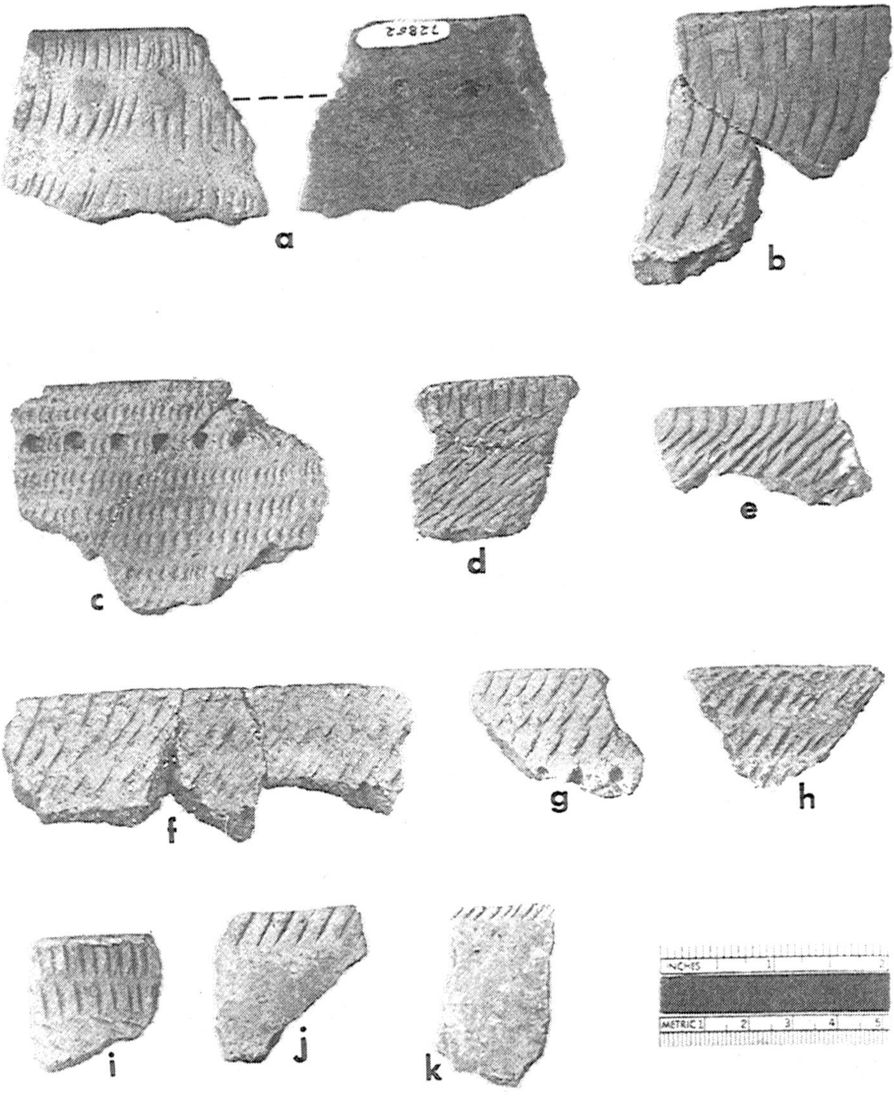

Laurel Linear stamp rim sherds from the Naomikong Point site.

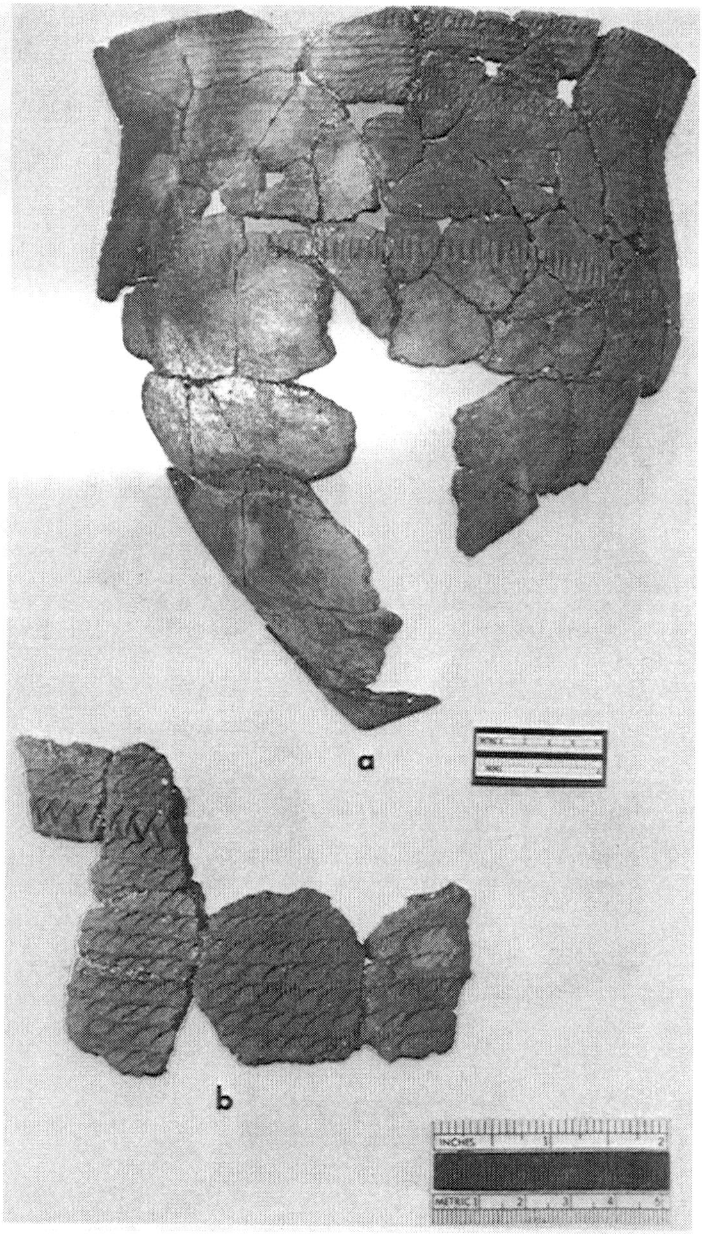

Comparison of vessel from Summer Island site with sherd from Naomikong Point site: *a*) Summer Island, *b*) Naomikong.

PLATE X

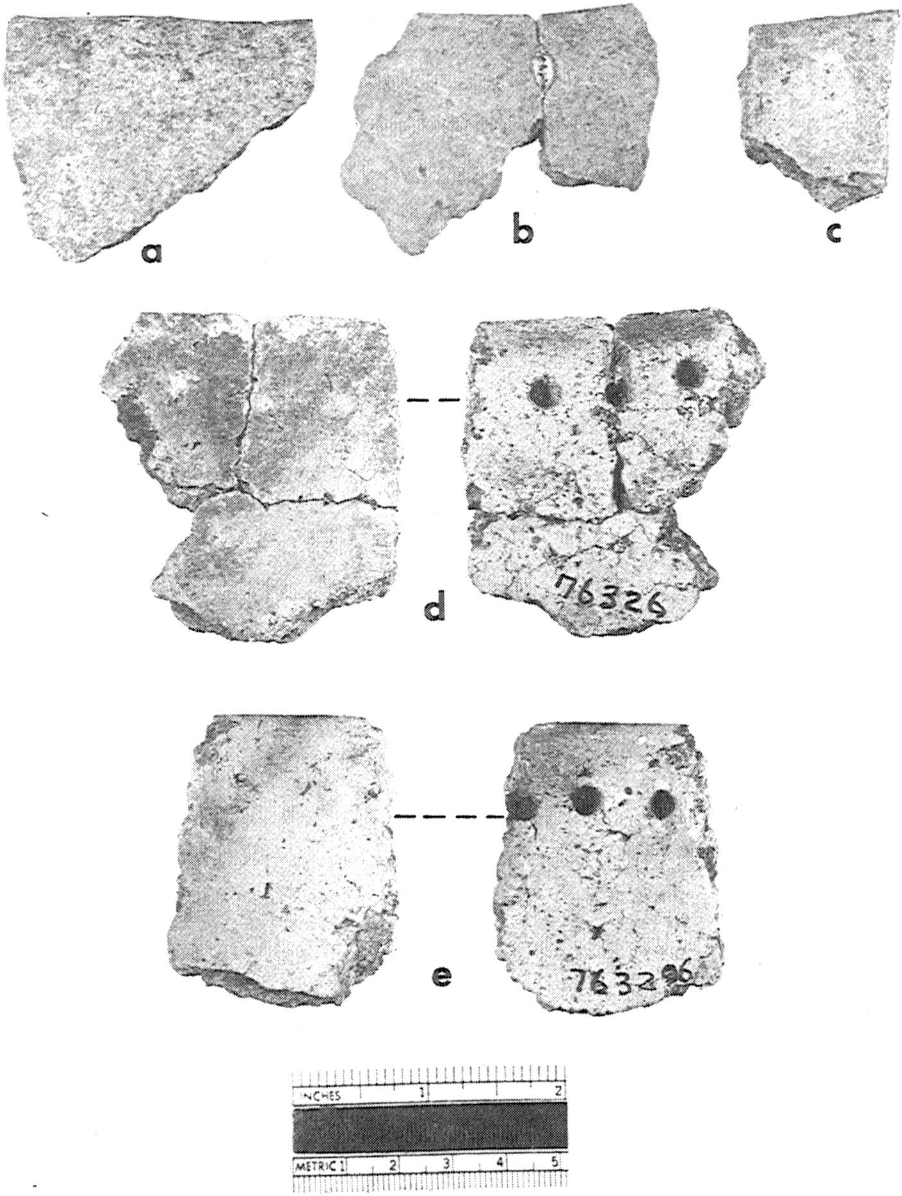

Laurel Plain rim sherds from the Naomikong Point site.

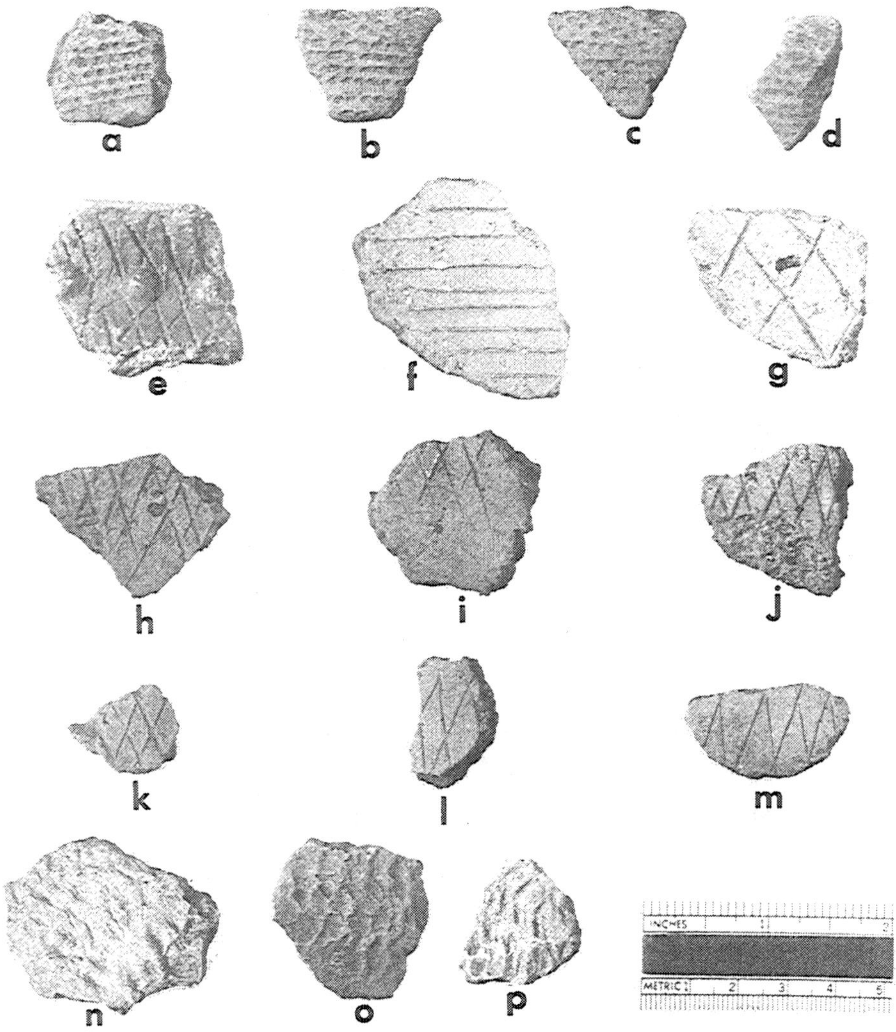

Laurel Dentate and Laurel Incised sherds; Incised and Fabric-impressed body sherds: *a–d*) Laurel Dentate, *e*) Laurel Incised, *f–m*) Incised Body sherds, *n–p*) Fabric-impressed Body sherds.

PLATE XII

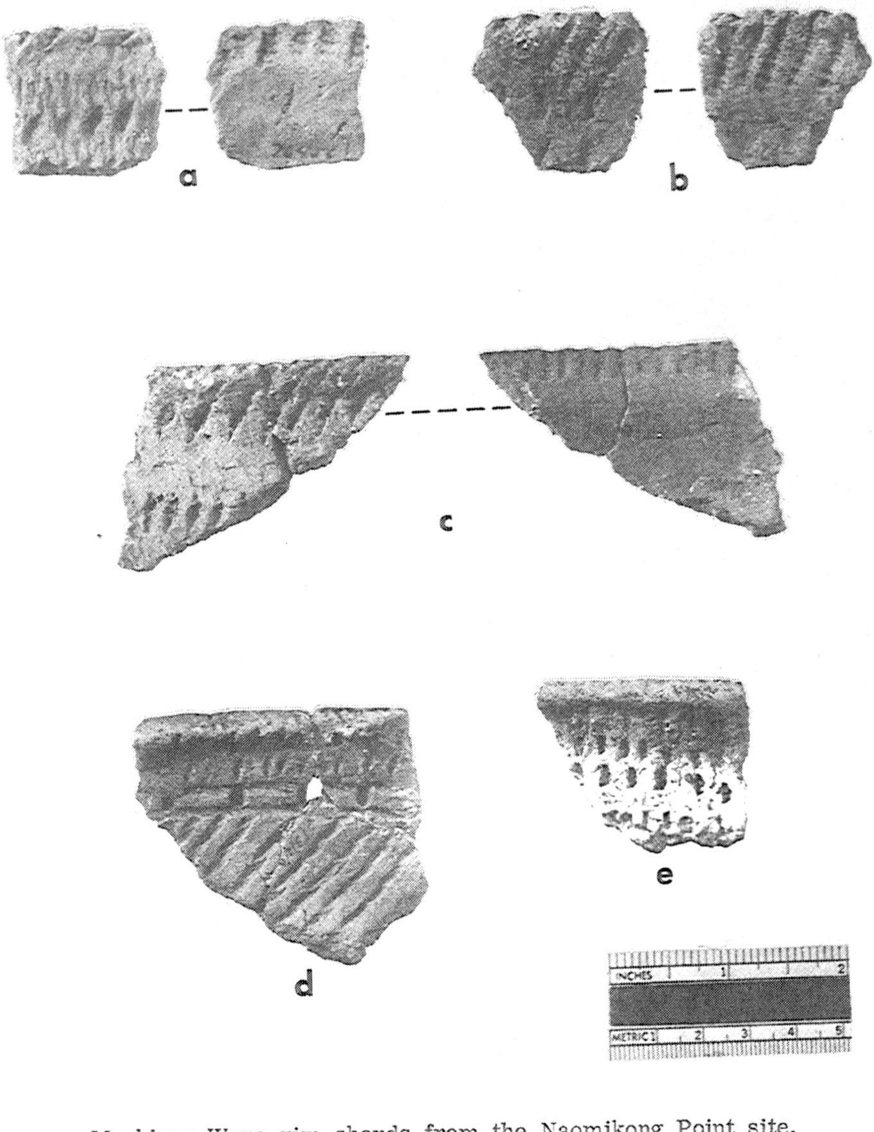

Mackinac Ware rim sherds from the Naomikong Point site.

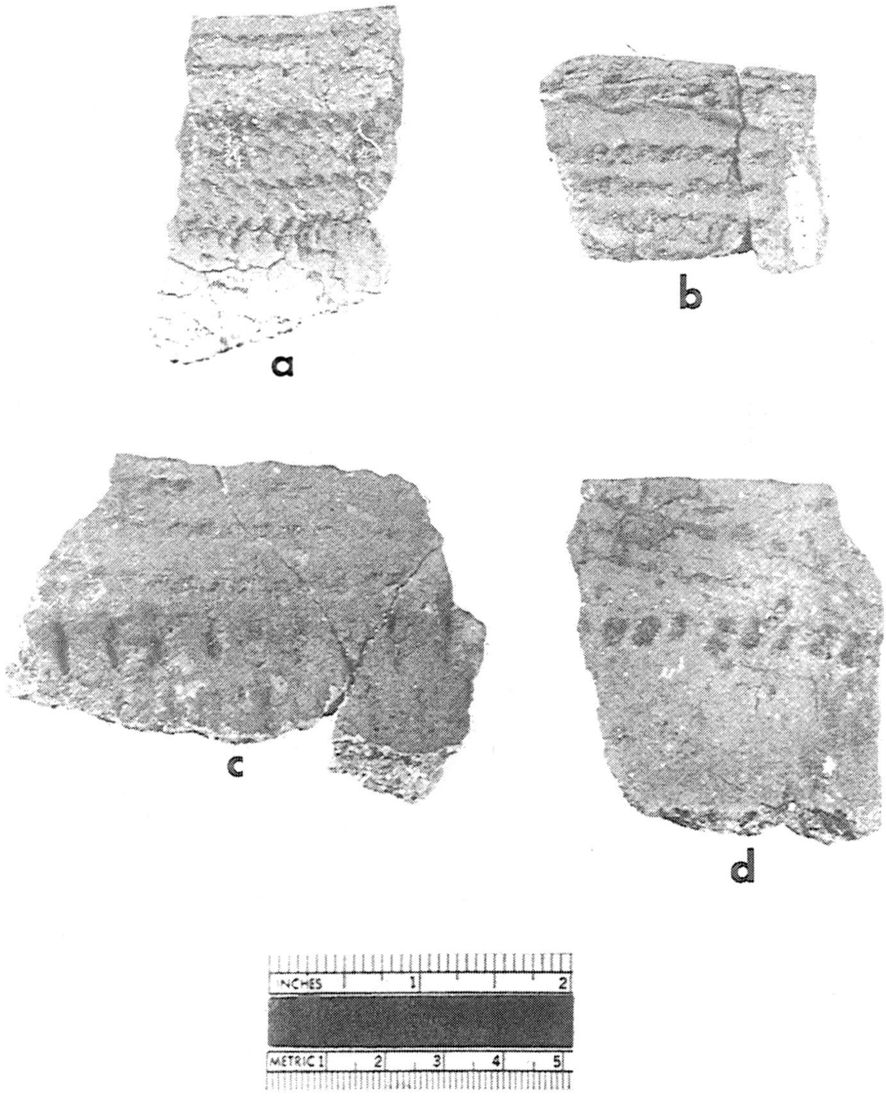

Late Woodland rim sherds from the Naomikong Point site: *a–b*) Bois Blanc Ware, *c–d*) Juntunen Ware.

PLATE XIV

a

b

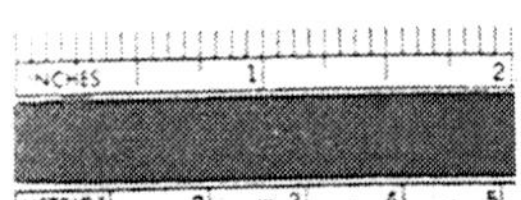

Mackinac Ware rim sherd and Huron Incised rim sherd from the Naomikong Point site: *a*) Mackinac Ware, *b*) Huron Incised.

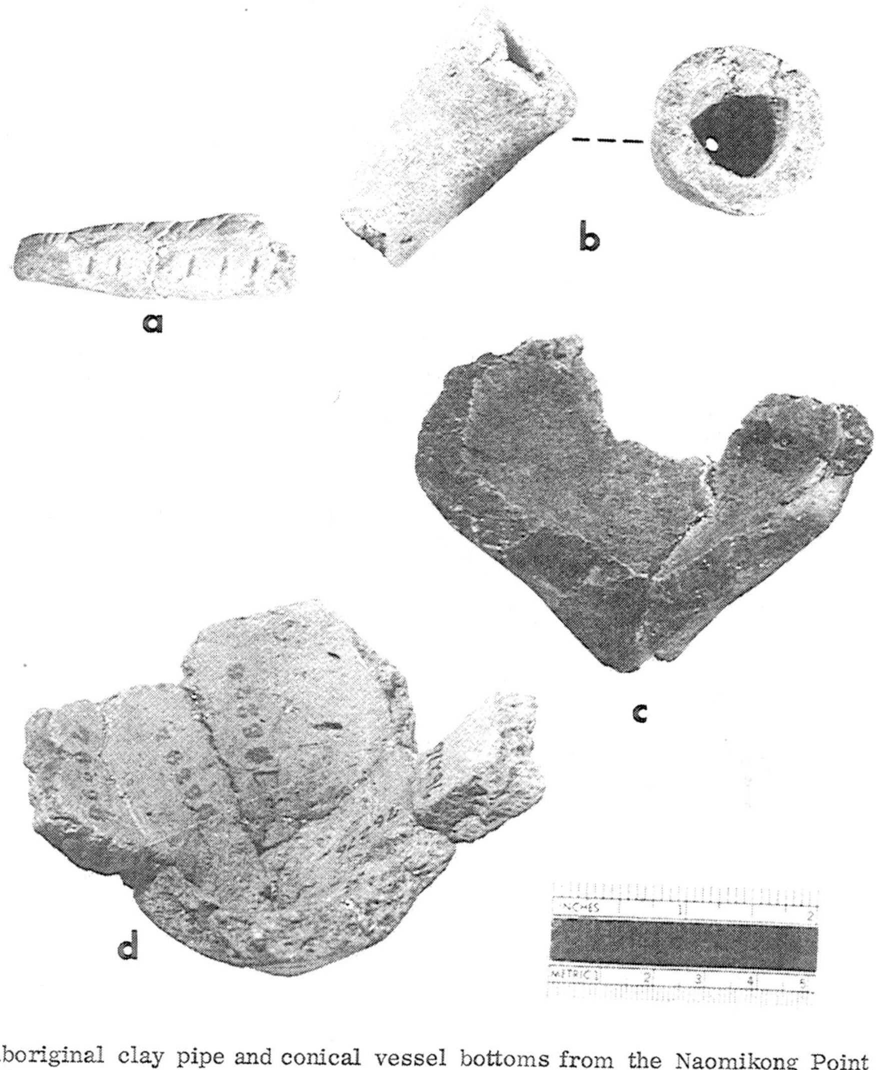

Aboriginal clay pipe and conical vessel bottoms from the Naomikong Point site.

PLATE XVI

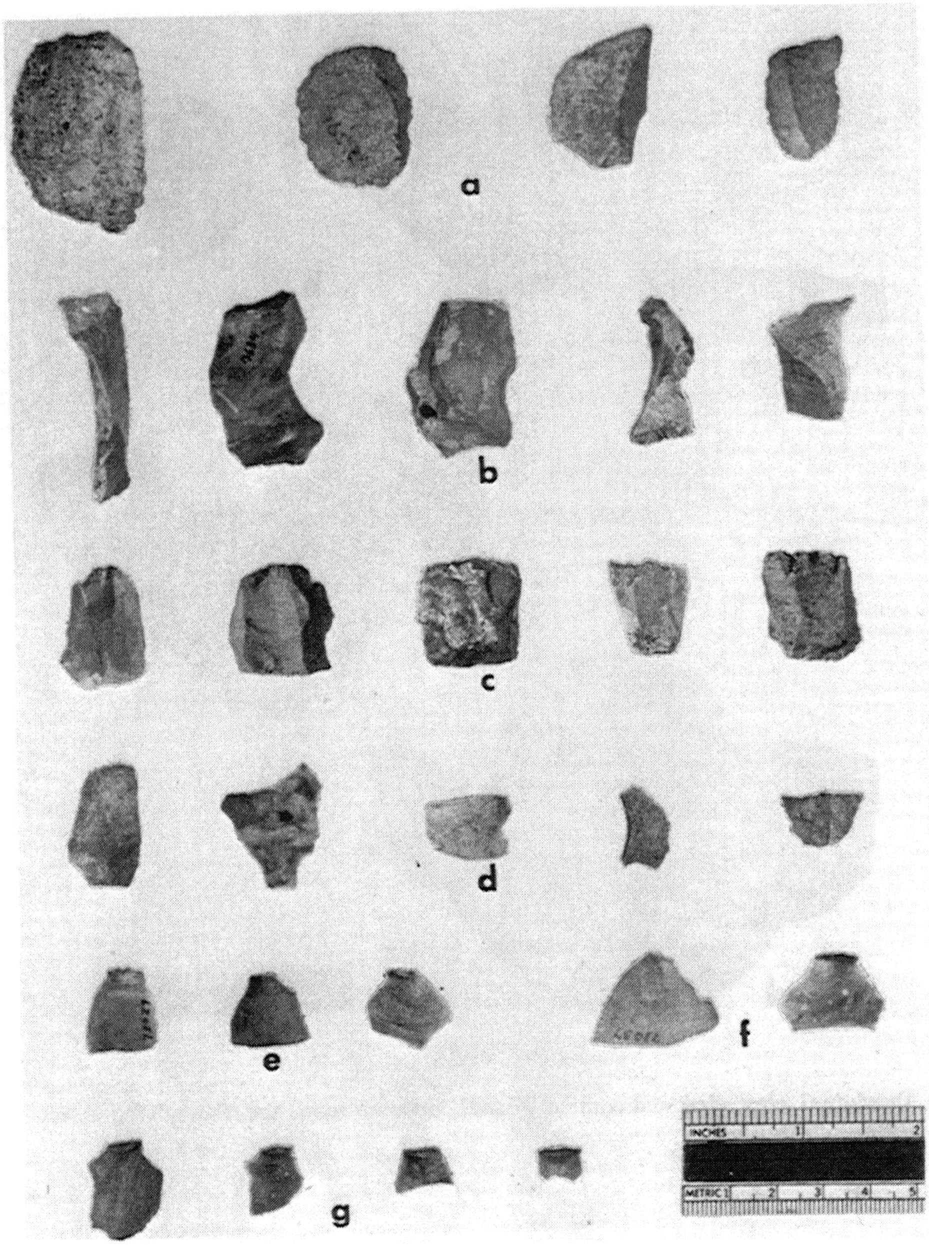

Chippage and core types: *a*) Decortication flakes, *b*) Block flakes, *c*) Bipolar cores, *d*) Flat flakes, *e*) Soft hammer flakes, *f*) Hard hammer flakes, *g*) Flakes of bifacial retouch.

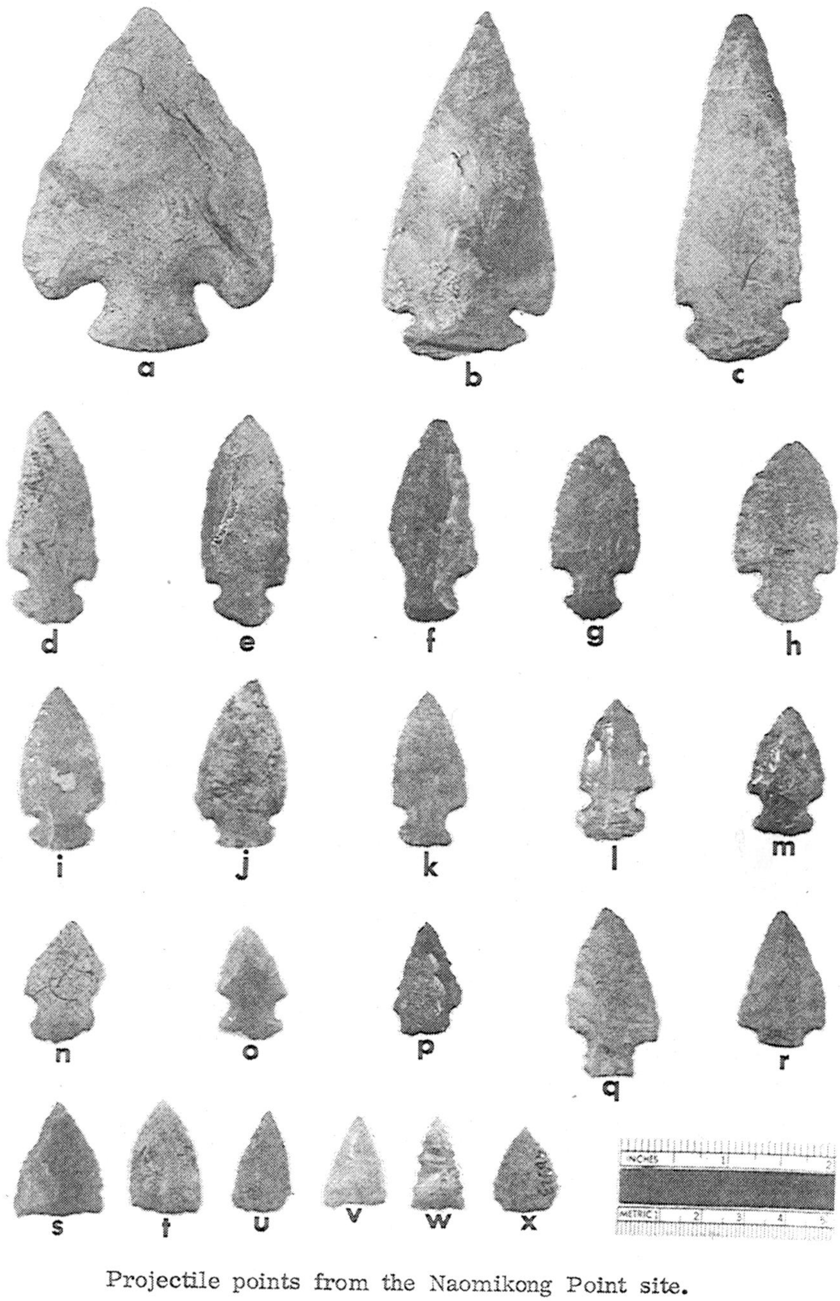

Projectile points from the Naomikong Point site.

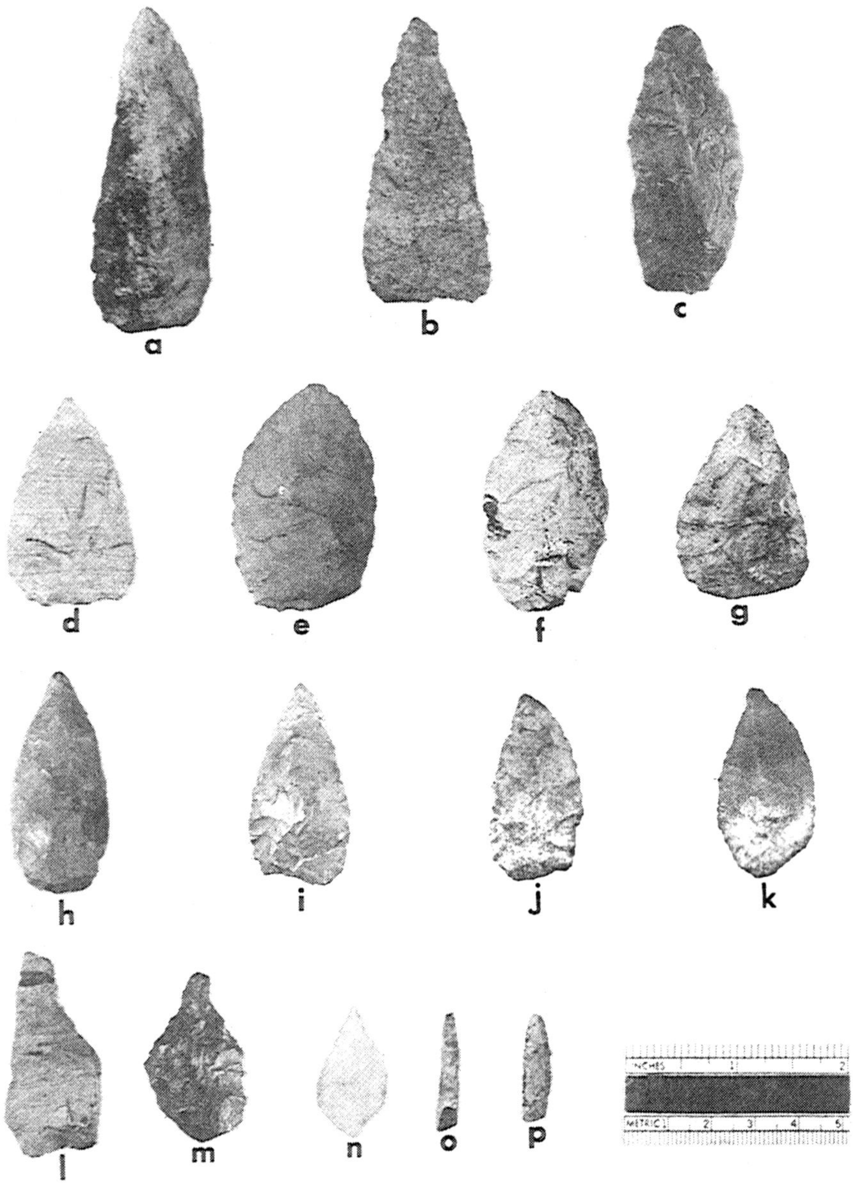

Preforms and drills from the Naomikong Point site: *a-k*) preforms, *l-p*) drills.

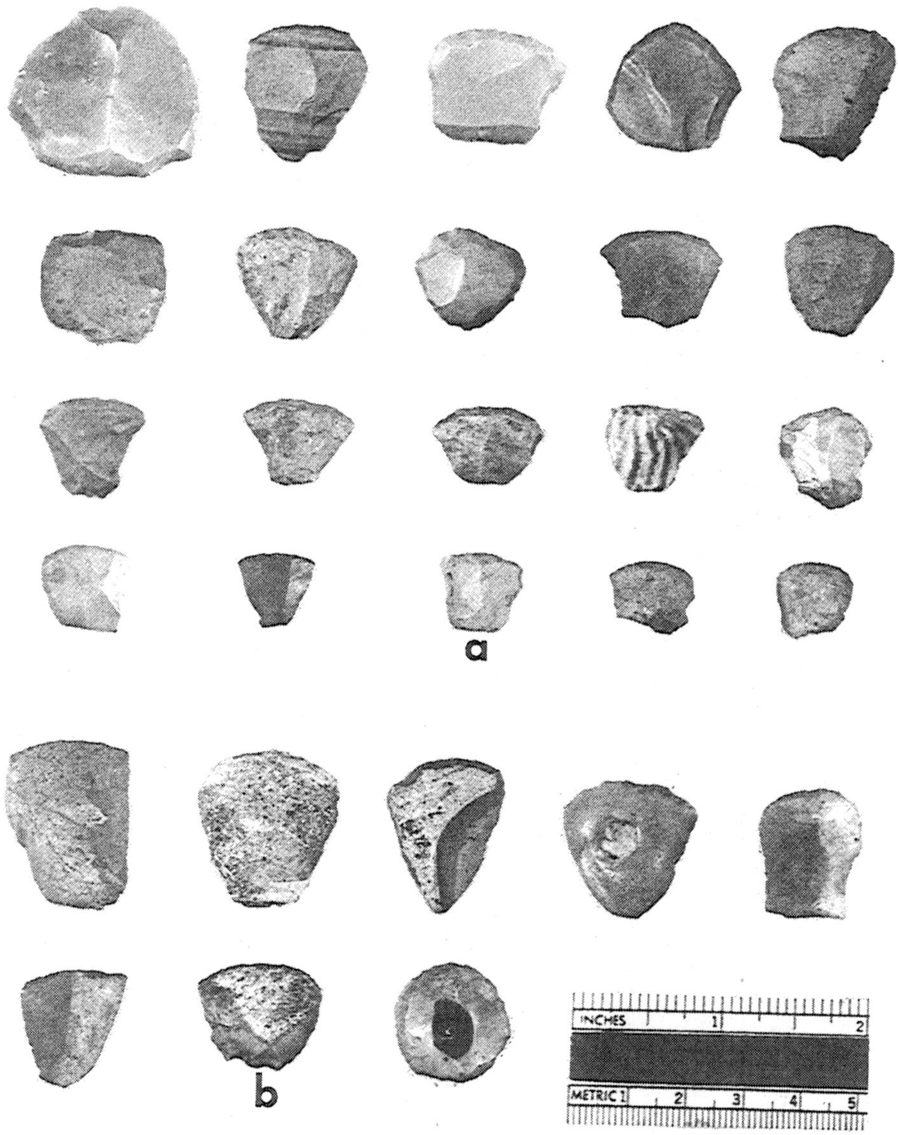

Scrapers from the Naomikong Point site: *a*) scrapers not made on decortication flakes, *b*) scrapers made on decortication flakes.

PLATE XX

Rough stone tools from the Naomikong Point site: *a–f*) net sinkers, *g*) celt, *h–i*) hammerstones, *j*) pestle.

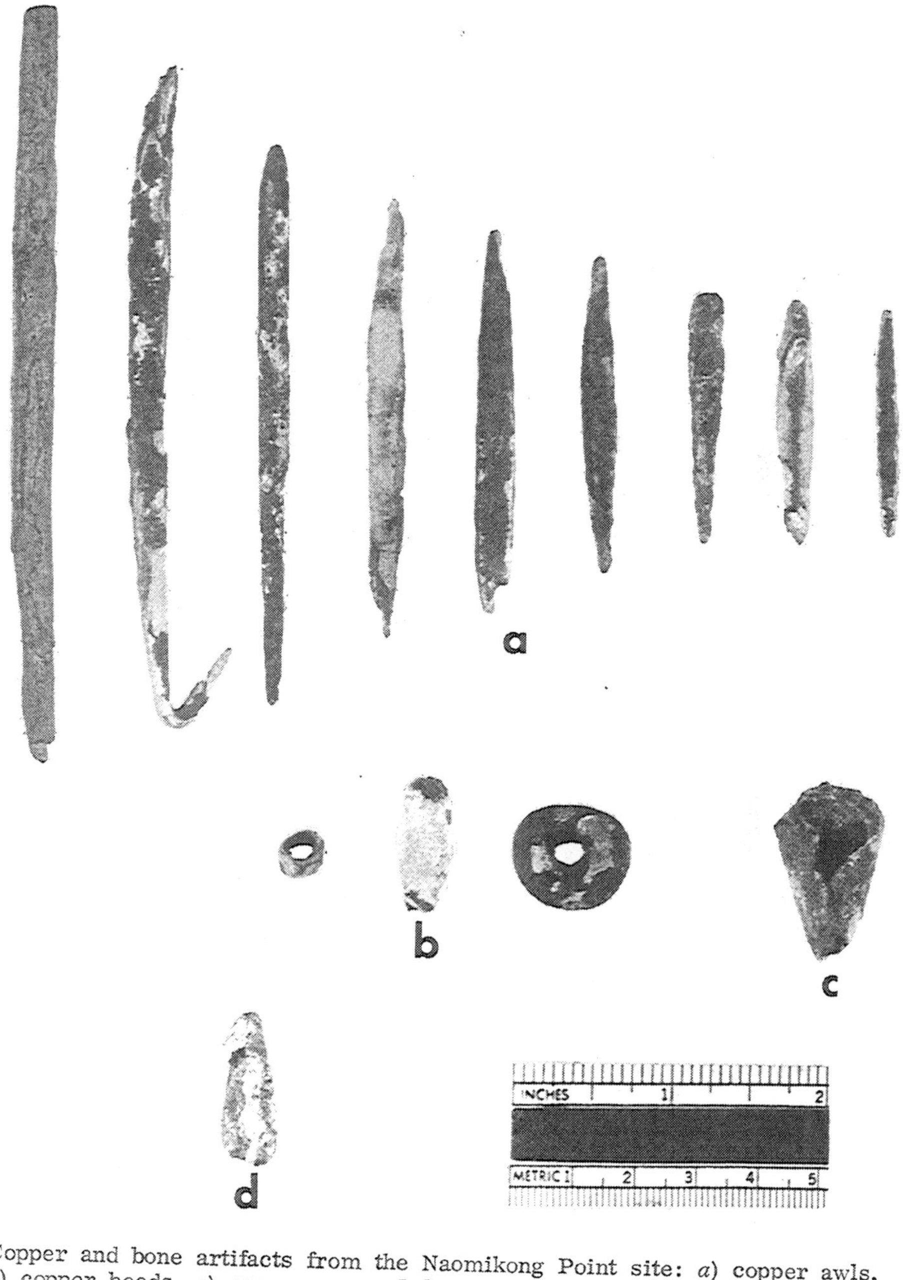

Copper and bone artifacts from the Naomikong Point site: *a*) copper awls, *b*) copper beads, *c*) copper cone, *d*) bone hook.